The Drama of Christmas

The Drama of Christmas

Letting Christ into Our Lives

Morton Kelsey

Westminster John Knox Press
Louisville, Kentucky

Scripture quotations from the New Revised Standard Version of the Bible are copyright © 1989 by the Division of Christian Education of the National Council of the Churches of Christ in the U.S.A., and are used by permission.

Book and cover design by Drew Stevens
Cover illustration: Mystic Nativity *by Sandro Botticelli. Courtesy of Superstock.*

First edition

Published by Westminster John Knox Press
Louisville, Kentucky

This book is printed on acid-free paper that meets the American National Standards Institute Z39.48 standard. ∞

PRINTED IN THE UNITED STATES OF AMERICA
94 95 96 97 98 99 00 01 02 03 — 10 9 8 7 6 5 4 3 2 1

Library of Congress Cataloging-in-Publication Data

Kelsey, Morton T., date.
    The drama of Christmas : letting Christ into our lives / Morton T.
Kelsey. — 1st ed.
        p.   cm.
    Includes bibliographical references.
    ISBN 0-664-25447-0 (alk. paper)
    1. Jesus Christ—Nativity.   2. Christmas.   I. Title.
BT315.2.K37   1994
232.92—dc20   94-8690

Acknowledgments will be found at the end of this book.

*To my wife Barbara
and my friend John Neary
who helped put
this book together*

Contents

Looking toward Christmas

Advent again,
and the very stones are silent.

In the east, no star;
only shadows
and the threat of darkness.
We have run out of light,
and we wait in fear.

   Still,

from the cosmic distance,
tentacles of brilliance probe,
seek us out, look for a dwelling place
   among us.

—Caryl Porter
Advent, 1990

1

The Mystery
of Christmas

Christmas is the most joyful and widely celebrated festival in Christendom. Wherever Christianity has been significant, the birth of Jesus of Nazareth has been a time of rejoicing and gathering to worship this newborn child. People who have not darkened the doors of a church for a year enter into the quiet mystery of a Christmas Eve service. It is true that as the Western world has become more secular, the Christmas season has been appropriated by the secular world. Still, in spite of the tinsel, sentimentalism and commercialism, something of the essential Christmas season persists. Men and women drop money into Salvation Army buckets, smile more readily as they walk down a crowded street, and even make efforts at reconciliation with those they have wronged. The ideal of self-giving love is in the air, and we give ourselves time to remember those who have tried to give us that kind of caring. The warm, human quality of the Christian holy day still remains. Warring nations declare cease-fire for the day. Families gather together. To most of our society it seems utterly wrong that, at Christmas time, any person should be alone or hungry or any child be without some gifts.

The Christian message has been the distinguishing quality of Western civilization for nearly two thousand years. Even though our conscious minds may reject the story of Christmas as history, or even be ignorant of what the day commemorates, a vein deep within our Western soul is touched and moved. As we see Christmas symbols in shop windows, hear Christmas carols over blaring loudspeakers, send out cards and decorate our homes, we hear an echo of the true meaning of the day. Try as we may, it is difficult to disown our Western Christian soul.

The resurrection of Jesus is certainly more central and indispensable to human hope than his birth. However, the events of the first Easter are so

1

transcendent and overpowering that they are difficult for most of us to grasp. In addition, in order to understand Easter and resurrection we have to pass through the ghastly brutality and torture of Golgotha. Not many of us can identify with the depth of crucifixion or the height of resurrection. Christmas, then, has become the most beloved of Christian feasts.

Nearly all of us can identify with the homey, utterly human scene of the newborn baby with the courageous, humble mother cherishing the miracle of new life before her. Joseph, her stalwart and faithful husband, stands behind the manger, his eyes big with joy. We can imagine the lowing and bleating of the animals in the stable, and the shepherds also fit right into this very human scene. In addition, we have seen the Wise Men, the Magi, often portrayed in song and picture; they add a totally different dimension to this picture. If the gloriously transcendent resurrection is one of the two poles of Jesus' life, Jesus' birth, with its simple, earthy humanness, is the other. Both are essential elements of the transforming life of Jesus. The birth narrative is the beginning of the greatest story ever told.

When I was a child, Christmas was a magic time for me, when life became what I longed for it to be. Children were important, presents appeared, the best meals of the year were prepared. I knew that this day was somehow related to the birth of Jesus, but I hadn't the vaguest idea what it meant. Santa Claus was somehow involved; I dictated letters to him and they were put by the chimney. Everyone was more pleasant during that time of year, and children were not told to be quiet and were not dismissed if some family rules were broken. I can still see the large tree with glass balls and real candles in little holders brushing the ceiling in one corner of the living room. (Only later did the twinkling electric lights appear.) I wrapped presents and helped Mother deliver them. On Christmas morning the presents were piled beneath the tree. Later in the day, my father read Dickens's *A Christmas Carol* and Van Dyke's *The Other Wise Man* in his deep, resonant voice as we gathered around the blazing fireplace. The fire blazed with many colors from the magic crystals we tossed into it. Christmas Eve and Christmas meals were straight out of Dickens, with roasted goose and plum pudding with a hard sauce that tasted like ambrosia.

A special Christmas service just for children was held at the little church just down the hill. An enormous glittering tree filled one side of the church; a crèche filled the other side. We sang wonderful hymns and then Santa Claus appeared and gave each of us a box of hard candy. All was well with the world. The whole Christmas holiday was permeated with warmth, love, playfulness, and beauty, an oasis of joy in a somewhat bleak childhood. My memories of those days seventy years ago are still vivid and clear. The poet, W. H. Auden, put it well: "Remembering the stable where once in our lives, Everything became a You and nothing was an It."[1]

Some adults, however, find Christmas disturbing and painful. Several psychologists and psychiatrists have described the problem as the Christmas neurosis—and it keeps them very busy right after Christmas Day. Many lonely and discouraged adults long to capture once again their childhood Christmas with its joy and hope and love; instead, though, the magic day turns out to be either empty or rife with bickering and dissension, and they crash and need help immediately. Their flickering candle of hope has been extinguished, and they wonder if they can go on.

Why does Christmas have such a powerful effect not only upon children but upon so many adults as well? Why does the birth of a baby two thousand years ago in an insignificant province of the almost-forgotten Roman Empire still grip those with a Christian heritage? What does Christmas really mean? Why is it so significant? Why do the events of this day form one of the basic foundations of the Christian faith? How can we capture their power once again?

For fifty years I have been meditating on the Christmas story in order to answer these questions for myself. I came to realize that in order to share with others the joy and hope revealed in the birth of Jesus, we need to be as clear as possible about what actually happened. So I began to live with the Christmas story, and the more I did this the more significant it became. In addition, the entire life and message of Jesus became much more clear to me. I began to see that the narrative of Jesus' birth was a perfect introduction to his life, death, and resurrection. I saw that the entire gospel story contains one basic message: The Holy One is essentially love.

God created the world and came into it in order to reveal the true nature of Divinity. Creating a world in which human beings might emerge and survive and relate to the Creator was an infinitely complex undertaking. Indeed, several of the most reliable scientific authorities have come to the conclusion that our world did not emerge by chance. They believe that the universe in which we live was created so that we human beings might exist and know and love our Creator.[2] They agree with Dante, who wrote of his vision of heaven in which he met the Love that moved the human heart just as it moved the sun and the other stars. The infinitely wise Creator knew that teaching human beings about the real heart of being would be difficult; it would take a great deal of time and patience to enable frightened, suspicious, self-centered human beings to believe that the Creator was love and that the Creator loved the least of us and wished to give us peace and growth, joy and eternal life. Jesus' life was the culmination of this lesson from the Creator.

How It All Began

Abram heard the call of the Holy One and took his family from Ur of the Chaldees to the land of Canaan. One of his grandchildren, Jacob, imperfect as he was, remained close to the God of his ancestors, and his family grew and expanded. To escape famine, this family took refuge in Egypt and grew to be a large and important nation; the Egyptians, however, made slaves of them. The Holy One of Israel rescued them and led them to the promised land and taught them a new way of life: They were to love their God with all their hearts and minds and souls, and they were to share that kind of caring with their neighbors.

Living in this way is very difficult. Like most of us, the people of Israel and their leaders were not disciplined or mature enough to follow that way. They neglected their God, who wanted to lead and guide them, and they mistreated their brother and sister Hebrews. Still, prophets and priests and many ordinary people remained open to the presence and message of God. They spoke out in the name of the Holy One of Israel, even though the kings and priests and most of the people persecuted them. Since the message was not getting through, however, God came among us as one of us; the Divine became flesh and dwelt among us.[3]

The infinitely wise God went to amazing lengths to create this unbelievably complex universe so that human beings might develop and live, so they might know and love their loving Creator. The divine wisdom also knew that if the Holy One appeared in full glory and numinous power, human beings would be so overawed that they would not retain their freedom; they would respond not from love but from fear. Like Kierkegaard's prince who fell in love with a peasant girl, God wanted to win human love by living as an ordinary person among ordinary people and truly winning their acceptance, and only then revealing the real nature of God. The Divine wanted to attract us, not overpower us. Thus the Christ, though he was divine, emptied himself, taking on the form of a slave, and was born as a human being.[4]

So God was born as a baby in a stable in Bethlehem of Judea. The divine light and love entered our troubled world, where peace was kept among nations only by the Roman sword. God wanted women and men to know the depth of the holy love in the heart of being, the love that moves the sun and the other stars. The message was this: Love is the ultimate reality and creator; live in harmony with this love and there will be peace on earth and goodwill among all people.

No wonder that even the faintest glimpse of the meaning of this event sets our hopes on fire. Creation was really not completed until this birth. The world into which Jesus was born did not like to be challenged by divine Love, so it tried to put out the light of love. At Jesus' birth the light overcame the darkness of the world, and later, when the world tried to utterly destroy the love made flesh, the light conquered once again and Jesus rose from the dead triumphant. The risen Jesus then ascended into the heaven that is both within us and beyond us and is now infinitely available to us. The celebration of the birth of Jesus still rings with such authenticity, even through the glitter and sentimentality of the Christmas season, because it reminds us that the loving Creator sought us out and came among us. There can be hope even in the greatest darkness when this idea becomes a real possibility for us.

Understanding and Imagination

The Creator made the incredible intricacy of the material world and also created the mysterious depth of our human knowing, our ability to perceive, to remember, to dream, to be open to God's presence and messages, and to love the Creator and one another. We can even be in touch with the vast realm that religious people all over the world call the spiritual domain and depth that some psychologists call the collective unconscious. We are indeed marvelously created both in our physical structure and in our capacity to experience, know, and love. We can experience both a physical reality and a spiritual reality, but we cannot truly understand either one unless we use our intellect, intuition, and imagination. Paul Feyerabend, a great student of the mysterious discoveries of nuclear physics, has written that we need to develop our imagination as much as or more than our intellect if we are to understand our physical world; the same holds true for the spiritual world. Discovery of either world requires careful observation, keen intellect, *and* vivid imagination.

There are two different kinds of imagination. In one we let our minds and thoughts soar; we observe whatever fantastic images come to us. This kind of imagination is not tied to physical reality. Another kind of imagination is related to the world around us and tries to understand it. Perhaps a spouse, child, friend, or stranger is unusually rude to us; we try to imagine what could be going on in that person's life that could cause such a response from a fellow human being. Historical imagination is of this latter kind. We place ourselves in another's place and time, and we ponder, picture, and imagine in what order certain events took place, why people of that time acted the way they did, and what message these happenings have for us today.[5]

It is difficult to believe what we cannot imagine. Amos Wilder has written that imagination is a necessary part of any profound knowing or celebration. Full engagement with life takes place only when imagination is engaged. We cannot understand those around us unless we put ourselves in their situation. We cannot be fully engaged either with the Eucharist unless we can imagine ourselves at the Last Supper or with Christmas unless we can picture what happened in Nazareth, Bethlehem, and Egypt.

In *Resurrection: Release from Oppression* I offered an account of what I believe actually happened in Jerusalem in A.D. 29, events that changed our world. In this book I follow the lead of W. H. Auden in his Christmas oratorio, *For the Time Being,* and of Dorothy Sayers in *The Man Born to Be King;* I present here a narrative of what I believe actually happened as the Holy One was born as a human being. I then add my own seventy years of reflection on the meaning of these events.[6] I am convinced that we can get the most from the Christmas story only as we enter into it with our spirit-guided imaginations and let it live within us.

Our ever-surprising Creator knew the depth and potential of the creatures that had been created. God also knew that human beings are far more touched and convinced by pictures, images, and stories than they are by abstractions, concepts, ideas, and logic. Since the messages and ideas and commandments had not broken through to the hearts of many of the Israelites, God so loved the world that the Holy One entered the fabric of human history as a human being and *revealed the mercy, love, and forgiveness at the heart of the divine Creator* in a way we human beings could understand.

In the small province of Palestine in the reign of the half-Jew Herod, God staged the greatest drama ever presented. God was the producer, the lead actor, and the prompter, and God even provided an audience. Divine providence carefully prepared a time and place in history and selected just the right characters for the divine drama. God's mysterious play was acted on a huge stage before the entire ancient world.

The cast, stage properties, and plot twists were numerous. They included Mary the daughter of Anne; Joseph and the baby Jesus; Zechariah and Elizabeth and John the Baptist; Caesar Augustus and his imperial taxation decree; the forced trip to Bethlehem and the donkey who carried Mary; the shepherds and the angels that appeared to them; the innkeeper; the stable; the Magi and their star; Herod and his court and soldiers; the dreams through which the Spirit and the angels spoke to many of the characters; the priests at the circumcision and Mary's purification; Anna; Simeon; the slaughtered children; the extras who were the people in Nazareth and the crowds in Jerusalem and Cairo. The scene shifts from Nazareth to Rome, from Bethlehem and Jerusalem to Egypt, and then back to Nazareth.

In order to enter fully into this drama I will first of all provide an orderly account of the birth and infancy of Jesus, using all the traditions found in the New Testament. (The notes at the end of the book will provide the evidence I have for the version of the story that I tell. When a legend fleshes out the story, I will note it as a legend.) Then we will enter the story and imagine what it would be like to be with each character who played a part in the greatest drama ever produced. We will try to understand each of them and the role he or she played in the unfolding story. We will meditate on the significance that each of these characters still has for us and our lives.

The coming of the divine Christ into the world is an incredibly important historical event; it happened in Palestine two thousand years ago. That is astoundingly good news, but the better news is that the same Christ seeks to enter the hearts of each of us today. Jesus' birth, therefore, is history—but it is also a parable, written in history about how God still seeks to enter the human heart. Our amazing God can be revealed both in history and in our souls. In his hymn, "O Little Town of Bethlehem," Phillips Brooks said it well:

> How silently, how silently,
> The wondrous gift is given!
> So God imparts to human hearts
> The blessings of his heaven.
> No ear may hear his coming,
> But in this world of sin,
> Where meek souls will receive him, still
> The dear Christ enters in.[7]

The resurrection and ascension of the human Jesus would have been impossible without his birth. Yet, the birth of Jesus would not have changed the world without the glorious resurrection. When I have finished sketching out the meaning of Christmas, I will then relate briefly the life, death, and resurrection of the adult Jesus. All through the story I will offer suggestions about how we can systematically open ourselves to the birth of the Christ in us.

2

A Savior Is Born

For thousands and thousands of years, nations and empires had risen and fallen in the cradle of civilization that stretched from Persia through Babylonia to Egypt and circled around the Black and Mediterranean Seas. These nations were constantly at war with one another. In addition, marauding bands of less civilized people swept down in waves from central Asia to seize and exploit what these civilizations had developed. Peace and security were the possessions of the powerful. Only after many centuries would real peace settle on this part of the civilized world.

The Stage Is Set

About a thousand years before the birth of Christ, the Hebrew people were led by Moses out of slavery in Egypt, and they took possession of the narrow neck of land known as Palestine. Their land was small, but important, as it was bounded on one side by the Arabian desert and on the other by the sea. Most of the trade routes from Africa to Europe and Asia passed through this land. By the power of their faith they subdued this land and built the city-fortress of Jerusalem. They developed a remarkable culture, one that still survives around the world, and a religion practiced by millions of people.[1]

The Jews also developed a magnificent written language, producing superb poetry as well as objective accounts of their nation's history, one of the first realistic histories written by human beings. This wonderful tool allowed the religious statements of their prophets to be recorded and handed down for posterity. These writings portray an increasing understanding that the Jewish people's God, Yahweh, was not only a national God, but *the* God who controlled the destiny of all human beings. Even in their captivity in Babylon they maintained both their literature and their faith that God was still with them. When the Persian conqueror set them free, the leaders of this people returned to rebuild Jerusalem and its Temple. When one of the Greek emperors tried to force them to defile the Holy of Holies in their Temple, the Jews revolted; they established their own sovereign nation again less than 150 years before the birth of Christ.

During the period that the Hebrews were gaining their sense of identity and deepening their religious convictions, the world around them was being transformed. Under the military genius of Alexander the Great, the Greeks conquered all the territory from Greece to India. But the Greeks never learned to work with one another, and Alexander's empire fell apart. After defeating Carthage, their only rival power, the Romans slowly gained control of Italy and Spain, of France and North Africa. Then the Romans turned east, and under the brilliant and enlightened leadership of Julius Caesar, the entire Western civilized world was united in one empire. (Julius Caesar made such an impression on his world that we still call his month of birth July, derived from Julius.) The Julian peace, however, lasted only for a few years. After Julius Caesar's assassination in 44 B.C., civil war broke out and raged until his heir, Octavian, or Augustus Caesar, gained control of the entire Western ancient world. The world peace of Octavian lasted much longer—many parts of the empire were peaceful for six hundred years, some of it for more than a thousand. (When we date a letter with August, we are paying tribute to one of the longest periods of peace in world history.) Shortly after the beginning of this era, Jesus of Nazareth was born, and during this era Christianity became a world religion. The right time had come, the time that Paul called the fullness of time.

There is more to this story. Herod, the king of Judea, who was an astute politician, was in control of Palestine. He became a close friend of Agrippa, Augustus's most trusted adviser and general. In the bloody civil wars fought for control of the empire, Herod had stood by Agrippa and Augustus. The empire rewarded him for his loyalty by officially recognizing his kingship and granting him regal authority in Israel. In addition, the empire accepted Judaism as one of the fully legitimate religions of the empire, without demanding that Jews acknowledge the emperor as divinity. Augustus also, out of respect for Herod's support in the strategic area of Palestine, passed this regal authority on to Herod's sons. Herod and his sons were to play an important part in the lives of John the Baptist and Jesus of Nazareth.

The Herald

The creative Spirit of God spun out our incredible universe and provided all the building blocks and direction necessary for the human race to emerge. These new creatures were able not only to understand the world around them but also to relate to other human beings and even to their loving Creator. Then God, as we noted earlier, called a special people who were taught to listen to the divine message and who were encouraged to live according to the Creator's vision for them. Divine providence then established one of the few eras of peace in human history so that the Creator's entrance into history could not go unnoticed. Finally, God sent a herald, a messenger, to prepare the hearts of the Israelites so that they would be more open to receive the Eternal One's entrance into time in Palestine.

Until I began to listen to the story of Christmas in depth, I did not fully realize that the story of Christmas begins not with Gabriel's message to Mary but with the conception and birth of John the Baptist to the previously sterile Elizabeth. (Throughout the history of Israel, God frequently brought forth leaders and prophets from women who had been barren. Sampson and Samuel were born of women who had been considered unable to conceive.)

Now, in the first years of the Augustan peace during the reign of King Herod, the priest Zechariah entered the Holy Place of the Temple. He was going to perform the ceremony of burning incense before the Lord by scattering the incense on hot coals that had been prepared there. But Zechariah was not alone; before him, at the right side of the altar of incense, an angel was waiting for him. As people almost always are in genuine encounters with the holy or numinous, Zechariah was startled, filled with awe, deeply moved. The angel, keenly aware of humans' awkwardness in dealing with an unexpected experience of naked holiness, hastened to reassure Zechariah that he had nothing to fear. Then the angel went on to say that he was God's messenger, sent to tell Zechariah that his prayers and those of his wife, Elizabeth, had been heard. His wife would conceive and bear not only a son but a very special child.

Zechariah and his wife were descendants of Aaron who took their obligations and opportunities as members of the priestly class very seriously; they belonged to a significant group of Jews who were earnest about their religion and practiced it faithfully and were looking for a savior to deliver Israel. However, Elizabeth was unable to bear any children, and they were old. In addition to having the natural human desire for children, the couple suffered because the Jewish people considered it a disgrace to be barren. Israel needed as large a population as possible if the Jews were to maintain their place among the nations surrounding them and to share their faith with other people throughout their world.

The message of the angel was even more overwhelming to Zechariah than the encounter itself. Zechariah could not believe the angel's words:

Your wife Elizabeth will bear you a son,
and you will call his name John.
And you will have joy and gladness,
and many will rejoice at his birth.

For he will be great before the Lord,
and he will drink no wine or strong drink.
And he will be filled with the Holy Spirit even from his mother's
    womb,
and he will turn many of the children of Israel to their God.

And he will go before the Holy One
in the spirit and power of Elijah
to turn the hearts of the parents to their children
and the disobedient unto the wisdom of the just,
to make ready for the lord a prepared people.

The astonished Zechariah replied with undisguised skepticism, "How can I be sure of such an impossibility? Both my wife and I are too old to have children." Only now did the angel reveal who he was, and he gave Zechariah a difficult sign to reprove him for his disbelief: "I am Gabriel; I stand in God's presence. I have been sent to speak to you and give you the good news, but you will be mute, unable to speak until the time that this occurs. These things will happen in due time."[2]

A large number of people usually gathered in the Temple courtyard to pray during the burning of incense. This ceremony was a particularly holy time, and since the priest usually went into the Holy Place for only a few minutes, the crowd wondered why Zechariah remained so long in the Temple sanctuary. When he returned, unable to speak to them, these devout Jews realized that he had seen a vision. Using sign language, Zechariah explained to the crowd that he had experienced a vision of an angel, but he kept the angel's message to himself. When his tour of priestly duty was completed, Zechariah returned home and Elizabeth became pregnant; she was overjoyed that the disgrace of her barrenness had been taken from her. As was the custom of that time and culture, and of many others, Elizabeth withdrew into the privacy of her home during her pregnancy.

The Angel Returns

At nearly the same time in the little town of Nazareth, a couple was preparing for their marriage. Joseph, a carpenter whose lineage could be traced back to King David, was marrying Mary, the young daughter of an old and devout Jewish family. Now, however, both families had been reduced to poverty. Many poor Jews like Mary and Joseph turned for hope and consolation to their faith. They followed the Mosaic law very carefully and went to the Temple as often as possible. The families of Mary and Joseph, as well as the families of Elizabeth and Zechariah (to whom they were related), belonged to a particularly devoted group of Jews known as the Anawin, the poor holy ones.

Marriage within the Jewish community consisted of two quite different ceremonies. First, Joseph had asked for Mary's hand, and he had offered a gift to her family. Then, after all the details had been arranged, the two families gathered together with the rabbi and two official witnesses and signed the contract of marriage. From that day on, Mary was legally Joseph's wife and sexual relations with another man would have been adultery. But Mary was very young and Joseph would not take her to live in his home for another year. Only then would the marriage be physically consummated.

In the sixth month, the month of Adar, roughly March in our calendar, Mary came back into her room after a meditative early walk in the garden. There before her stood a messenger of the Holy One. The angel spoke to her immediately, and once again the message was even more startling than the numinous presence: "Greetings, favored one! The Lord is with you." Mary was puzzled, overwhelmed with awe. Although she had been raised in a deeply religious household, she had not thought of herself as more than an ordinary, sincere young Jewish woman. She did not understand what was happening. The angel hastened to allay her fear and awed confusion:

> Do not be afraid, Mary, for you have found favor with God. And now, you will conceive in your womb and bear a son, and you will name him Jesus. He will be great, and will be called the Son of the Most High, and the Lord God will give to him the throne of his ancestor David. He will reign over the house of Jacob forever, and of his kingdom there will be no end.

In wonder and astonishment, Mary replied to the angel: "How can this be, since I am a virgin?" The angel then spoke amazing words, telling Mary that this child would be a child of the Most High: "The Holy Spirit will come upon you, and the power of the Most High will overshadow you; therefore the child to be born will be holy; he will be called Son of God."

The angel went on to tell Mary that great events were taking place in Israel: "And now, your relative Elizabeth in her old age has also conceived a son; and this is the sixth month for her who was said to be barren. For nothing will be impossible with God."

Unlike Zechariah, Mary never doubted the angel's words, and she knew full well what her fiance might think, what her family would fear, what the world would say. Nevertheless, looking directly at this holy messenger of the Most High, looking indeed into the heart of holiness, Mary was willing to sacrifice everything else and she made her simple and profound reply: "Here am I, the servant of the Lord; let it be with me according to your words."[3] The angel was waiting for a response, for the Holy One never forces holiness on anyone. In a blaze of joyful glory the angel disappeared. The vision was over.[4]

Before Joseph completed the second part of Jewish marriage, he discovered Mary was pregnant. That Mary could have committed adultery seemed utterly impossible, yet facts were facts. What was he to do? Joseph belonged to the poor holy ones. He was a very devout Jew. He did not wish to condemn Mary, but on the other hand he did not see how he could live with someone about whom he carried such doubts. Listening to his inner doubts, Joseph decided to break the marriage contract, which he had entered so joyfully. He would do it with as little public notice as possible. He realized how difficult this would be for Mary. Auden describes these nagging, persistent doubts:

Joseph, you have heard
What Mary says occurred;
Yes, it may be so.
Is it likely? No.

Mary may be pure,
But, Joseph, are you sure?
How is one to tell?
Suppose, for instance . . . Well . . .

Maybe, maybe not.
But, Joseph, you know what
Your world, of course, will say
About you anyway.[5]

Joseph's plan was interrupted by the dream-vision of an angel. The messenger sent by the Most High was very direct and spoke with divine authority: "Joseph, son of David, do not be afraid to take Mary as your wife, for the child conceived in her is from the Holy Spirit. She will bear a son, and you are to name him Jesus, for he will save his people from their sins."[6] When Joseph awoke from his sleep, the vision of the angel still burned within him, and he knew that this had been a true dream. Joseph immediately took Mary into his home; the marriage was complete. But he did not have any sexual relations with Mary before the birth of the child. Now that they were living as husband and wife, they talked together and found that angels had told both of them to give the same name to the child Mary carried in her womb. As these bewildering events unfolded, Joseph acted with extraordinary grace, fully earning Auden's admiration: "To do what is difficult all one's days / As if it were easy, that is faith. Joseph, praise."[7]

Strange as these events seem to us, however, the Jews themselves should not have been surprised, for their scriptures contained many examples of such happenings. Centuries earlier, Isaiah had written, "Look, the virgin shall conceive and bear a son, and they shall name him Emmanuel."[8] In Jesus, the Divine is uniquely with us and one of us; that is the meaning of the name "Emmanuel."[9]

A Time of Great Hope

Shortly after Mary had settled into her new home, the couple decided to visit her relative Elizabeth and to share their mysterious good news with her. Joseph and Mary made careful preparations for the long journey to the home of Zechariah in one of the many villages in the mountainous country around Jerusalem. The meeting was sheer joy and ecstasy. At Mary's greeting, the baby in Elizabeth's womb jumped for joy. In a moment of prophetic inspiration, Elizabeth burst forth with these words: "Blessed are you among women, and blessed is the fruit of your womb. Who am I that the mother of my Lord should come to me? For behold the moment your greeting sounded in my ears, the baby in my womb jumped with gladness. Fortunate is she who believed that the Lord's word to her would find fulfillment."

In response to Elizabeth, Mary spoke out of the depth of her soul. Poetically and prophetically she proclaimed the essence of the hope of Israel and its coming realization through the child within her, who would bring a wonderful, radical, awesome, mysterious message from which would spring real Christianity:

> My soul proclaims the greatness of the Lord,
> and my spirit has found gladness in God my savior:
> Because He has regarded the low estate of His handmaid—
> for behold, henceforth all generations will call me fortunate.
> Because He who is mighty has done great things for me.
> And holy is His Name,
> and His mercy is from generation to generation
> on those who fear Him.
> He has shown His strength with His arm;
> He has scattered the proud in the imagination of their hearts.
> He has put down the mighty from their thrones
> and has exalted those of low degree.
> He has filled the hungry with good things,
> and the rich He has sent away empty.
> He has helped His servant Israel
> in remembrance of His mercy,
> as He spoke unto our fathers,
> to Abraham and his posterity forever.[10]

After this ecstatic encounter, the two women embraced and settled down to talk about lesser things—about Mary's move to Joseph's home and her journey with Joseph to Elizabeth and Zechariah's home. Joseph and the mute Zechariah, meanwhile, communicated as best they could. Mary then joined Elizabeth in getting a meal for the four of them. The next morning Joseph set off on the rigorous journey back to Nazareth. The three months passed quickly, both women doing the daily chores and talking with one another about the mysterious graciousness of God. Just before the birth of John the Baptist, Joseph returned to Zechariah's home and took his wife back to Nazareth.

Except for Mary and Joseph, none of their relatives or friends knew of the glorious hope that was growing day after day in the hearts of Zechariah and Elizabeth. But the time came when they could hide it no longer. Elizabeth gave birth to a healthy baby boy. The whole village rejoiced with the parents of the child; God had shown incredible mercy to their revered friends.

Eight days after the birth, relatives and friends gathered for the holy rite of circumcision. This ceremony made the child a full member of the chosen people, the Israelites. At this service the child was given a name, just as Christian babies are given a name at baptism. The priest who performed the rite and all the people who attended the ceremony assumed the parents would follow Jewish custom and give the baby his father's name, but hearing what they were about to do, Elizabeth spoke up: "No, you can't do that. His name will be John." Since the villagers knew one another well, their families having lived together for generations, they argued with Elizabeth. When she would not listen to these relatives and friends, they turned to the mute father and asked him what the child was to be named. He asked for a writing tablet and astonished the whole gathering by writing: "John is to be his name." And then Zechariah could speak again.

His first words were inspired by the Holy Spirit and brought awe to all their neighbors and relatives. He spoke like one of the great prophets of old. The people could hardly believe what they heard, and they wondered what destiny this child might have. The words they heard flowing from Zechariah's mouth filled them with awe and hope:

> Blessed be the Lord God of Israel,
>   for he has looked favorably on his people and redeemed them.
> He has raised up a mighty savior for us
>   in the house of his servant David,
> as he spoke through the mouth of his holy prophets from of old,
>   that we would be saved from our enemies and from the hand of all
>   who hate us.

Thus he has shown the mercy promised to our ancestors,
    and has remembered his holy covenant,
the oath that he swore to our ancestor Abraham,
    to grant us that we, being rescued from the hands of our enemies,
might serve him without fear,
        in holiness and righteousness
        before him all our days.
And you, child, will be called the prophet of the Most High;
    for you will go before the Lord to prepare his ways,
to give knowledge of salvation to his people
    by the forgiveness of their sins.
By the tender mercy of our God,
    the dawn from on high will break upon us,
to give light to those who sit in darkness and in the shadow of death,
    to guide our feet into the way of peace.[11]

It is no wonder the people were astonished, for many of them knew the deep darkness of brokenness and oppression, and some of them sat in the shadow of death. These words gave them much hope and comfort, and the words have continued to give comfort down through the ages as people have continued to read or to sing them.

Zechariah and Elizabeth provided the home and religious atmosphere in which this child could grow in strength of spirit and body. In time he was led out into the wilderness, where he began to call the people of Israel to repentance and baptism. He was indeed a herald preparing the way for the one who was born shortly after him. People came from all over Palestine to hear his message and change their lives. They were prepared to follow a prophet who would lead them into the kingdom of heaven.

The Birth and Naming of Jesus

Mary and Joseph had settled into their home in Nazareth and were preparing for the birth of their child. The fact that they had entered the second stage of marriage so early caused comment in the little town of Nazareth, but they were happy there. Then Augustus Caesar overturned their plans by ordering a census of his empire. Augustus needed a great amount of money to keep peace within his empire and to defend its borders, and he also had an ambitious building program in Rome; it was impossible to estimate the money available for these projects without a registration of all taxpayers. (Registration of a population was tantamount to taxation.) In order to make sure that the census was accurate, Augustus demanded that each adult male be enrolled on the records in his own tribal village. This meant that Joseph had to go to Bethlehem, the city of David, because he belonged to the family of King David.

Governments do not take excuses or wait. Even though Mary was nine months pregnant, Joseph and Mary had to get ready and leave for another arduous trip from the northern part of Galilee to the central part of Judea; this was ninety air miles, and many miles more on the road that snaked through the rough mountains of Palestine. The trip took them from near sea level to Mount Zion, nearly three thousand feet in height. The couple gathered together provisions for the trip and clothes for the baby, and they packed these supplies in bags for their donkey to carry. Then they started up toward Jerusalem and Bethlehem. The trip had been easy nine months before. However, now it was winter and the winter rains had begun, and in the passes there was snow. And Mary was nine months pregnant. The journey took them nearly a week.

When they arrived in Bethlehem, they realized that the time for the baby's birth was on them. They desperately needed a place to stay as the sun sank below the horizon. But all the lodgings were full. At last they found a cave that a farmer had converted into a stable. A wooden shelter had been added in front of the mouth of the cave; it increased the cave's size and kept out the elements. In the back of the stable the farmer had piled hay for the animals that needed shelter. In this rugged place Mary gave birth to her infant child. The parents washed the baby and then wrapped him in the strips of cloth that they had brought along for that purpose. They felt very much alone—though a legend tells of an orphan child lying far back in the stable-cave, who came out to fetch water for them.

They were not alone long. Nearby there were shepherds watching their sheep in the cold Judea night. Just as an angel had told Mary that she would bear a very special child, so now another angel appeared to the shepherds, the lowest of the lowly, people despised because they could not obey the Hebrew Law. The numinous majesty and light, the glory of the Divine, shone around them. They were terrified. The angel knew their fear and quickly reassured them and spoke words of great hope and comfort to them: "Do not be afraid; for see—I am bringing you good news of great joy for all people: this day in the city of David a Savior is born who is Messiah and Lord. And this will be your sign: you will find the baby wrapped in strips of cloth and lying in a manger."

Then the full glory and grandeur and splendor of heaven surrounded and encompassed the shepherds. A multitude of the angelic hosts began exalting God with immortal words of praise: "Glory to God in the highest heaven, and on earth peace and divine good will to human beings."[12] The numinous vision faded; the angels returned to their heavenly realm.

When the dazed shepherds recovered, they began to urge one another to go to Bethlehem and find this Savior who cared about shepherds and came to them in a manger in a stable. Such a Savior would understand them and their plight. They gathered their flocks and made their way as quickly as they could to search for this newborn child. They crossed the fields and found the stable just as the angel had described it. They poured out to Mary and Joseph the story of what they had experienced. They could hardly find words to convey the power of their marvelous vision of the angelic hosts and of the incredible good news the divine messengers had proclaimed. As they knelt before the child, they sensed the same wonder they had felt in the angel's presence.

The shepherds lingered in the stable with the baby and the mother and father. Then they returned to their fields with their sheep. The next day and for many days after, they were praising and glorifying God as they told the story to people in Bethlehem and the countryside near it. Most of those who heard their story were amazed, but they found it hard to take seriously a story told by ignorant shepherds. Finding so little response, most of the shepherds soon stopped talking about what happened to them. Eventually, most of those who had shared in the angelic visitation did not even remember their moment of power, hope, and insight. But Mary added the experience of the shepherds to her memories of the other mysterious events that had happened to her; she pondered these things in her heart and wondered what the future might bring for her and her child.

Eight days after Jesus' birth, Mary and Joseph took Jesus to be named and circumcised. This was a very important ceremony for Jews. As with John the Baptist, circumcision made Jesus a member of the nation and religion of Israel. Jesus was a Jew, and he was raised in the religion of his ancestors; he had to be rooted in one culture in order to speak to all cultures. Contrary to the community's expectations, he was named not Joseph but Jesus, a name that means "Yahweh helps/saves" or "God's salvation."

The Presentation of Jesus
and the Purification of Mary

Jesus' parents remained in Jerusalem because they were near the Temple in the holy city. This enabled them to present Jesus there and to receive the rite of purification for Mary. According to the Jewish law, every firstborn male child was consecrated to God and released from service in the Temple by the payment of five shekels to the Temple; also according to the Law, every woman who gave birth to a child had to come to the Temple for purification. The woman and her husband offered either a lamb or two pigeons to the priest as a sacrifice for her. According to the Law, women were unclean until this sacrifice was offered.[13] Mary and Joseph followed the Law meticulously.

While Mary was being purified and Jesus, the Son of God, was being presented to God, a man named Simeon, led by the Spirit, entered the Temple court and took the child in his arms. He was another of the devout, poor holy ones, and he had been promised that he would not die until he had seen the Messiah, the consolation of Israel. He blessed God, and words of praise and thanksgiving poured from his lips:

> Mighty Master, now you may let your servant depart
> in peace, since you have kept your word.
> For my eyes have seen this salvation
> that you made ready in the sight of all people:
> a light to be a revelation to the Gentiles
> and to be a glory for your people Israel.[14]

Both Mary and Joseph were astonished by Simeon's actions and words.

Still holding the child, Simeon turned to the parents and blessed them; then, turning to Mary, he spoke a mysterious oracle to her: "This child is destined for the falling and rising of many in Israel, and to be a sign that will be opposed so that the inner thoughts of many will be revealed—and a sword will pierce your own soul too."[15] These words gave Mary even more to ponder in her heart.

At that moment a woman of great age came up to them: Anna of the northern tribe of Asher, who remained in the Temple courts praying night and day and fasting. She had been a widow for many years and was considered a prophetess. She heard Simeon's words and the spirit of prophecy came on her; she began to praise God and to speak about the child not only to Mary and Joseph but to all who were in Jerusalem. It was now time for Jesus and his parents to return to Nazareth, but the arrival from the East of Magi at the court of Herod threatened their lives and forced them to flee as refugees to Egypt.

The Coming of the Magi

Late in King Herod's reign and after the birth of Jesus, three Magi from the East came to Jerusalem. They were searching for a child who was to become the king of the Jews. All over the city they asked the same question: "Where is the child who has been born king of the Jews? We have seen a new star as it rises over the horizon and we have come to pay him homage."[16] Such words would have caused some notice at any time. Also they were spoken by men of great wealth who were deeply versed in the ancient lore of the stars and dreams. The question they asked, therefore, caused a real stir in Jerusalem, especially since the people of the city knew how paranoid Herod was about anyone who might seek to replace him; he had even killed his beloved wife and two sons when he feared they were plotting to take away his throne.

Herod's agents soon brought him news of three men asking treasonous questions. The idea of a messiah was in the air, and messiahs took precedence over kings. Herod called the chief priests and leaders of the Pharisees together. He asked them where the Messiah was to be born. "Bethlehem" was the unanimous answer of these religious leaders of Israel, and they quoted their scripture to validate their response:

And you, Bethlehem, in the land of Judah,
   are by no means least among the rulers of Judah;
for from you shall come a ruler
   who is to shepherd my people Israel.[17]

Armed with this information, Herod arranged to have the Magi secretly meet him. He learned everything he could from them, and then he shared with them his knowledge of the Messiah's probable birthplace. Then, lying through his teeth, he told them: "Go and search diligently for the child; and when you have found him, bring me word so that I may also go and pay him homage."[18] The Magi set out immediately even though it was evening. They saw the star appear over the horizon and followed it until it came to rest over the place where the child was lying. They were overjoyed when they entered the house and found the child with Mary, his mother; their quest had not been in vain.

They knelt down before the child, as people did in that day in the presence of royalty. Then they opened their treasure chests and brought forth their precious gifts. It was customary in those days for people to bring gifts when they visited and paid homage to kings and emperors, and the Magis' gifts were fit for a king: gold, frankincense, and myrrh. Their lore about the stars, their intuitions, and their dreams had led these Gentiles to the birthplace of the new king. They were deeply satisfied; they were filled with hope as they gazed on the holy child. They then returned to their lodgings and slept well except for a dream that warned them about Herod's intentions. The Magi left early the next morning and disappeared into vast deserts to the east.

The Rage of a Tyrant

The time had come for Joseph, Mary, and Jesus to return home, but the very night the Magi departed, Joseph had another warning dream. The angel of Yahweh spoke an urgent message: "Get up, take the child and his mother, and flee to Egypt, and remain there until I tell you; for Herod is about to search for the child, to destroy him." Well aware of Herod's violence, Joseph awakened and alerted Mary. Together they made ready to take flight immediately. They disappeared into the night toward Egypt, political refugees in search of asylum, just as, throughout the centuries, many other Israelites had fled to Egypt when they were persecuted. Tradition has marked with an ancient church, St. Sergius, the place where they lived in Cairo. Thus, Mary, Joseph, and Jesus fulfilled the prophecy spoken many centuries before: "Out of Egypt I have called my son."[19]

When Herod realized that he had been duped by the Magi, his rage was uncontrollable. He sent for the military and gave his orders, which were brutal and clear: "Go to Bethlehem. Find all the male children under two years there and in the country around that city, and kill them." (He had learned from the Magi the approximate time that the child would be born.) The soldiers did their grisly job. Sorrow and tears drenched Bethlehem. The Jews had experienced many times such senseless destruction; Jeremiah, for example, had long before cried out:

> A voice was heard in Ramah,
>   wailing and loud lamentation,
> Rachel weeping for her children;
>   she refused to be consoled because they are no more.[20]

So loud was the weeping in Bethlehem that it could be heard miles away in Ramah.

Herod had been foiled again by God's messengers; he did not eliminate the feared child. Not much later, after Herod became violently ill, wasted away, and finally died, the faithful messenger of God blazed forth in Joseph's dream and told him Herod was dead and it was safe to return home.[21] Joseph gathered his family and their belongings and set out for Judea. When he arrived there, he discovered his country had been divided among Herod's heirs. The violent Archelaus was now king of Judea. In spite of the attractiveness of Bethlehem, and of Jerusalem with its Temple, they followed the guidance of an angel and returned to Nazareth in Galilee.

Joseph and his family made their home there once again, and Joseph took up his vocation of carpentry. When Jesus was only four or five, Joseph took him into the shop with him and began to teach him the trade of carpentry. Jesus also learned to read and write Hebrew at the synagogue; he learned Greek and Latin so that he could deal with the customers who came from the Greek city of Sepphoris just a few miles away. We hear little of Jesus until he went down to the Jordan to be baptized by John the Baptist, but we do know of one incident that occurred when he was twelve. Jesus' family, along with other faithful Israelites, went up to the Temple for the Passover. After a day or so of their return journey to Nazareth, Mary and Joseph realized Jesus was not in their company. They had to return to Jerusalem, where they found him in the Temple talking to the priests. Jesus returned home with them and grew in wisdom and stature, and in divine and human favor. When Joseph died, Jesus the carpenter supported his family until he was called to public ministry.

3

Mary

Many people in our Western world have known Christianity only from the outside or have been brought up in churches that teach Christianity as a dull set of prohibitions and restraints. Nothing could be further from the truth. The Christian story is a wild, fascinating story of the Divine entering our constricted and difficult human lives. One may challenge the Christian message as untrue, but it is anything but dull or boring.

Mary, who holds the center stage in the first act of the cosmic drama, is the most universally revered feminine figure in the history of our world. Followers of Islam listen to the Koran's praise of her faith and chastity. Roman Catholics pay homage to her as Queen of Heaven, and Orthodox believers venerate her as the Mother of God and the only human being ever to be fully divinized; she achieved the full spirituality possible for a human being. Many Protestants also have begun to appreciate this amazing woman who bore Jesus in her womb and then mothered him without interfering with his spiritual destiny. Mary did not just give birth to Jesus and raise him, she also was at the crucifixion and the empty tomb, and she was in the upper room with the disciples waiting for the Holy Spirit to come to them at Pentecost.

Few religious scenes touch us more or have been painted more often than that of the baby Jesus with Mary and Joseph in the stable in Bethlehem. How peaceful, happy, and serene the Madonna looks as she holds the Christ child in her arms, her embroidered robe and her azure veil glowing with a pure, unearthly light. Even the crude, unkempt stable with its animals has an idyllic beauty. The stalwart Joseph stands behind the mother and child, a symbol of stability and trust. This picture of human and divine birth stirs a deep, responsive chord in us as a sense of peace and goodwill permeates our hearts.

Yet if we truly enter into the scene, we see more than just its romantic joy. Mary had traveled a rough road to get to this austere place, and her journey was to become even more difficult before she knew the consummate joy of Easter and Pentecost. Many medieval paintings of the Nativity have a small but distinct crucifix hanging on a rafter of the stable, a disconcerting reminder of what Mary and her son would confront. Most of Jesus' followers would endure persecution and death over the next three hundred years, and many other followers of this divine child have throughout the ages experienced similarly brutal hostility. It is valuable, then, to look at this nativity scene from Mary's point of view. Bearing the Son of God was infinitely rewarding for Mary, but also very difficult. Mary reminds us of the courage, openness, and patience it takes to incorporate the wondrous gift of Christ into our hearts.

The Annunciation

Most of us think we might like to have an encounter with a friendly angel. We forget that any such encounter strikes humans with a combination of awe, wonder, and terror. An experience of a real angel would be like looking over the edge of the Grand Canyon for the first time and seeing below us the ageless rocks laid out in a vast panorama; we would feel tiny and insignificant, a mere fragment of both space and time. An angel—an awesome, mysterious, numinous reality—would give us a feeling of the ineffable Holy, and we would need to be reminded in any such encounter that we have nothing to fear. The Holy not only gives humans an overwhelming sense of being loved but also makes demands on them just by appearing to them. I knew one man who started a practice of praying and keeping a journal and was making great progress, and then he stopped; he told me he had seen some light, and he didn't like it.

Mary had no preparation for the visit of the angel Gabriel. She had not considered herself in any way unusual; she was an ordinary young woman, only thirteen or fourteen years old, who was about to marry a carpenter. She had followed the religious law of her people, and she went to the synagogue on the Sabbath. She had gone with her family to Jerusalem for many Passovers; she meditated on the psalms and read the scripture daily. She had ministered to the need of those in her village less fortunate than she. She helped her mother in the household and learned what was expected of every young Jewish woman. Perhaps it was just because she did not feel special or unusual and lived her faith so implicitly that the Holy One selected her.

She was shaken and startled by the presence of the holy messenger. The angel then told her that she would bear a child and would call him Jesus. This child would be called Son of God and would reign over God's people forever. Mary did not doubt that the Holy One could use her as an instrument of the divine will; she only wondered how this could happen to a virgin. Then the angel answered her with his mysterious words about the Holy Spirit coming upon her and the power of the Most High overshadowing her. Gabriel went on to tell her that her relative Elizabeth, who was considered barren, had conceived. Mary replied with her immortal words: "Here am I, the servant of the Lord; let it be with me according to your word."[1] How many of us have been able to give ourselves into God's hands with this kind of confidence? Mary was ready and willing to do and be whatever God needed of her. Bringing *any* child into the world is an awesome responsibility, but Mary was told that she would give birth to no less than the Messiah, the Son of God. And Mary was willing to accept. What humble courage!

Have you ever tried to imagine what this overshadowing of the Divine must have felt like to Mary? In his poetic play, *For the Time Being*, W. H. Auden describes what an incredible experience the annunciation might have been for her. Auden's Mary says:

> What dancing joy would whirl
> My ignorance away?
> Light blazes out of the stone,
> The taciturn water
> Burst into music,
> And warm wings throb within
> The motionless rose:
> What sudden rush of Power
> Commands me to command? . . .

> My flesh in terror and fire
> Rejoices that the Word
> Who utters the world out of nothing,
> As a pledge of His word to love her
> Against her will, and to turn
> Her desperate longing to love,
> Should ask to wear me,
> From now to their wedding day,
> For an engagement ring.[2]

Of course Mary told Joseph of her angelic visitation, and soon it would be visibly obvious that the power of the Most High had indeed overshadowed her. Let us imagine how Mary and Joseph looked at their amazing situation and then follow them in imagination to the hill country near Jerusalem and then to Bethlehem and Egypt. Joseph was torn by doubt, and Mary was alone in a hostile world; she must have been deeply hurt to realize that Joseph could not believe her story. Her family would have been even less understanding. I wonder how long it took the wound of

Joseph's doubt to heal in her. Joseph was making plans for a divorce when he experienced a messenger of the Most High in a dream. He realized how wrong he had been, and he took Mary into his home. He was awed by what had happened, and they made their plans together for the child's birth.

Gabriel had graciously told Mary about her cousin Elizabeth's pregnancy, and Mary realized that Elizabeth was someone who would understand her own mysterious situation. Mary and Joseph set off immediately for Zechariah's home; they made the long journey in the beautiful Palestinian spring. It was a relief for them to be away from Nazareth and its gossips, who had been wondering why Joseph had taken Mary so suddenly into his home. Joseph was happy to leave Mary with someone who could truly empathize with her. The following day Joseph returned to Nazareth. When the two women met, their spirits poured out their visions of hope. In Elizabeth and Zechariah's home Mary was able to become comfortable and secure with her vision and with the baby growing within her. Mary's song of praise about how the world would be turned upside down came from the same spirit that had impregnated her. We cannot reread these words often enough when we have lost hope for God's loving presence in the world. After magnifying the Holy One of Israel, Mary sang:

> He has shown strength with his arm;
>   he has scattered the proud in the thoughts of their hearts.
> He has brought down the powerful from their thrones,
>   and lifted up the lowly;
> he has filled the hungry with good things,
>   and sent the rich away empty.[3]

Billions of human beings revere Mary, and most people who recognize the name of Augustus know the name only because Mary gave birth to her son during his reign. This fact is a vindication of Mary's prophecy; God's will, beautifully proclaimed by Mary, has been done.

Three months Mary remained with Elizabeth and Zechariah, friends and kinfolk who believed her, encouraged her, and loved her. They could even share the messages the angel had given them, and they looked forward together in expectation of what the mysterious future might bring. Then, just before the birth of John the Baptist, Joseph returned and brought Mary home from Judea to Nazareth. There Mary was at peace, and she prepared to bear the Son of the Most High.

The stories of the time Mary spent with Elizabeth and Zechariah and of the birth and circumcision of John give us a picture of the best of Jewish religious and family life. God had prepared a people who loved each other, who were open to the Spirit, who were nourished by their religious ceremonies and rituals. It is no small matter that Mary had people like Elizabeth and Zechariah to whom she could turn and with whom she could integrate the meaning of her overpowering religious experience. We need one another if we are to understand our most profound visions of the Holy. Today, unfortunately, the churches are few in which we are encouraged to share the religious experiences that many of us have.[4]

The narratives of the birth and naming of John depict village life. At the baby's circumcision and naming, Elizabeth and Zechariah's neighbors argued with Elizabeth about the name that she proposed for the child. Only when Zechariah confirmed the name by writing on a tablet would the neighbors accept the unusual practice of naming a child by other than the father's name. Then Zechariah opened his mouth and in the spirit spoke his prophecy, known as the Benedictus, words that have been as meaningful to Christians down through the ages as the words of Mary. No wonder that the people of the hill country of Judea were struck with awe as the Spirit of God spoke through Zechariah as it had through the prophets of old. His words resonated with their hopes:

> By the tender mercy of our God,
>   the dawn from on high will break upon us,
> to give light to those who sit in darkness and in the shadow of death,
>   to guide our feet into the way of peace.[5]

Despite her inner peace, Mary was faced with a difficult task as she took up her daily activities in Nazareth. Most people are more comfortable with violence than with unconventional sexual behavior, and Mary's neighbors were no exception. The villagers could count, and they talked about the impropriety of Mary's pregnancy. They smiled knowingly as Mary passed them to draw water at the village well. When the story of a heavenly visitation leaked out, they snickered openly. Some of the more charitable nodded wisely and said that she had always been a little odd, but they had never thought this of her, poor child.

What has the secular world said about Mary down through the ages? It has mocked and laughed and snickered just as the villagers did, and it pronounced its verdict about Mary's child: illegitimate. Bearing the Christ child was not an easy destiny for Mary. Most of the saints who have tried to bear the Christ in their hearts have suffered ridicule and condemnation before they were finally accepted. Whether seen or unseen, a crucifix always has hung in the Christmas stable.

The decree of Augustus Caesar was a blow to Mary and Joseph. They had to go to Joseph's town of birth to register for the census despite Mary's pregnancy; Rome made no exceptions. They already had made their plans for the child's birth and had prepared a corner of their home for the baby. But instead of being with their family and friends for the baby's birth, they had to travel over a hundred miles to Bethlehem. They had to set off in a very few days. Since there was no public transportation and only the rich had carriages, Mary was forced to ride a donkey that Joseph used to carry heavy beams. They dug up their little hoard of silver denarii with Augustus's image on it, and they gathered the necessary clothes for the trip and for the baby. Mary was nearly nine months pregnant.

They received the news on Monday, and Joseph completed the jobs he had contracted to do. They closed up their little house. As soon as the Sabbath was over and it was religiously legal for Jews to travel, they set out with enough bread, wine, and cheese to sustain them for several days. The first day of the week, Sunday, was a cold and wintry day, and the wind was raw and biting; people traveled as little as possible in Palestine at that time of the year. As night fell, there was no village in sight. Imagine what Mary felt, how tired she was; she had ridden twenty miles on a donkey's back, and no village was in sight. As soon as the sun went down, the road was alive with bandits. The tired couple could not go on into the night. Turning a bend in the road, they came to a mill set beside a little stream, the miller standing in the doorway. They inquired if there were any place where they might spend the night. The miller looked on the couple with compassion, remembering that his people once had been slaves in Egypt and had wandered homeless for many years.

The miller knew it was dangerous to take in strangers, but hospitality was considered a great virtue. He told Mary and Joseph they might sleep in the storeroom next to the mill among the bags of grain. They were deeply grateful; they slept soundly and were wakened in the morning by the miller bringing them fresh round loaves of bread and hot milk. Joseph thanked him profusely. He and Mary washed in the icy millstream, ate their food, and then were on their way.

About noon on Monday the wind came up, dry and bitter, blowing from the desert slopes of Arabia. The couple's lips were dry and chapped; sand bit their faces and stung their hands. When they stopped for a bite of bread, they could find no shelter. All day long they pushed on. Often Mary let her eyes close and her head drop upon her breast. They finally arrived in Samaria; Joseph knew they must have a warm place to stay. As Jews, however, they were unwanted in Samaria, and all households were closed to them. Since the country is often kinder than the cities, Joseph finally found a rural place where caravans stopped. For an exorbitant price they had a dingy little room.

On the third day of travel, Tuesday, heavy and threatening clouds came with the dawn. Mary hated to leave the dismal but at least bearable quarters; a small brazier had warmed them through the night. They needed to travel another twenty miles that day under leaden, ugly skies. The naked, rugged peaks looming up on either side of them made the road look cruel and oppressive. Since the day was very short, one of the shortest of the year, they were still far from a village when the light began to fail. A shepherd took note of them as they plodded down the road and came up to them. They could scarcely believe his words: "You must go no further. The passes ahead are a lair of robbers. Come with me to the sheepfold and rest until morning." They gladly accepted his offer and followed him. After eating some dry bread with the wine the shepherd gave them to wash it down, they were directed to a corner of the shelter. There they found a pile of sheepskins, and they slept warm and comfortable between the skins spread on the ground as the fire crackled through the night.

In the morning the shepherd tried to persuade them not to go on. The rain had begun to fall during the night. A thousand little rivulets ran across the road, and in places the mud was deep. But they had to reach Bethlehem. So all day long they plodded through the rain. In the passes, the rain turned to flurries of snow, which blurred their sight, and the melting flakes chilled their sodden clothes. Joseph found it difficult to lead the donkey through some of the mountain streams that flooded across the road. Finally they arrived in Bethel, whose name means "house of God"; Jacob had named it after his vision there of a ladder to heaven, and it had remained a holy place. Cold and wet, Joseph and Mary found a lodging where pilgrims stayed. The innkeeper took advantage of their plight and asked for most of the remaining coins they had.

On the fifth day of their journey, Thursday, they awakened to the clear cold weather that so often follows rain in desert countries. As they set out for Bethlehem, Mary was bundled up in all the cloaks she had. Still she was cold; the bitter wind penetrated to her bones. Her hands, like Joseph's, ached from the frigid wind. The couple passed around Jerusalem, and as the sun was setting, they saw the village of Bethlehem etched against the golden sky. They were certain that there they would find a place to spend the night. Furthermore, Mary knew that her time to give birth was drawing near. She was exhausted—she had just spent five long days and more than a hundred miles on donkey back. Considering that at about two weeks before birth the baby drops in the womb, sitting on a donkey for such a long time must have been truly uncomfortable for Mary.

They had little money left, but Joseph sought out a pilgrim's lodging place. The host opened the door. Behind him a fire blazed on the hearth. The man shook his head—no room in his lodging, but there were some stables down the road. None of the villagers would open their doors to the persistent knocking of the frightened, tired travelers. Joseph knew he must find some lodging very soon. He spotted a shed built against a rock, and behind the shed he found a warm cave with animals and clean straw—a stable. It was there that the Son of God was born; the stable was his home and a manger was his crib. The baby was born, and they wrapped him in the strips of cloth they carried with them and laid him in the clean straw of an animal's feeding trough.

What incredible courage Mary had. Bearing the Christ child was no easy task. When we ask to have the Christ born within us, we would do well to reflect on how difficult it was for Mary; and this was only the beginning of Mary's journey.

Starting that very night, and lasting for several weeks, Mary and Joseph were given marvelous confirmation of the importance and destiny of the child Mary brought into the world in Bethlehem. Mary and Joseph were gazing in awed joy at the mystery of human birth that lay before them when they heard a commotion outside the stable. Then the door of the shed was thrown open. A dozen shepherds, young and old, fell in adoration before the child. The shepherds told them of an angelic visitor who had announced to them the birth of a savior child and where to find him. Then, the shepherd continued, a multitude of angels had appeared to them, speaking of peace and joy and goodwill among all people. They found everything just as their vision had described it, a baby in swaddling clothes lying in a manger. The shepherds lingered and then departed, praising the Holy One for the revelation they had received.

At the solemn ceremony of circumcision a week later, Jesus was named and integrated into the fabric of Jewish religion and society. In the days that followed, Joseph enrolled before the Roman authorities in Bethlehem. He, his wife, and their infant son finally found a place to stay in the town where they could live more comfortably. They decided to remain there until Mary's purification at the Temple. They were required to present Jesus before Yahweh and at the same time to pay the five shekels the law demanded. So the Holy One was presented to the Holy One in the Temple. Both parents were stunned when the aged Simeon came up to them, took Jesus in his arms, and spoke prophetically of Jesus' saving mission not only to the Jews but to the Gentiles as well. Neither Joseph nor Mary had told anyone of their visions, and yet this wise man seemed to know the whole story. Simeon addressed Mary with strange and alarming words: "This child is destined for the falling and the rising of many in Israel, and to be a sign that will be opposed so that the inner thoughts of many will be revealed—and a sword will pierce your own soul too."[6] Scarcely had Simeon ceased speaking when one of the holiest women of Jerusalem, Anna, the daughter of Phanuel, came up to the holy family, praising God. She prophesied that this child was the Messiah and would bring about the redemption of Jerusalem.

Mary kept all these strange events in her heart and constantly pondered what they might mean. God breaks into the hearts of all of us in unexpected and wonderful ways, but if we do not reflect on them in the light of our Christian heritage, their meaning may be lost. Mary is our human model and mentor: She meditated at length on her life, which was crammed full of "contrasting experiences of expectation and disappointment, ordinariness and upheaval, joy and fear."[7]

Sometime in the midst of these experiences the most unusual event of Jesus' birth occurred. Three Magi from the East appeared at the family's dwelling. The rich attire of these men was travel-worn and stained, but their bearing revealed their importance in the world. They had followed a star and had been led to this place where the child lay. They were looking for a king who would bring peace to the world. Their determination and wisdom were obvious; their gifts of gold and frankincense and myrrh were gifts worthy of a king. Again, Mary and Joseph were astonished, but the visitors showed them the star that stood over the place the child was sleeping. The Magi departed, and it was time for the family to return to their home in Nazareth. An angelic messenger, however, appeared to Joseph and warned him of Herod's fear and rage.

As soon as Joseph awakened from his dream, he and Mary gathered what food and other necessities for the baby they could find; then Mary again climbed onto the donkey and the family fled into the night. It was bad enough making the trip to Bethlehem, but now they feared the worst. Sixty miles separated them from the border of Herod's kingdom and safety. Mary, Joseph, and the baby were displaced persons, refugees from political oppression. Each time they heard the sound of hooves on the desert road, they hid behind a rock or a mound of dirt. By dawn they had made their way to Tekoa, and they hid during the day. They feared every soldier they saw, every official. At night they made their way to Hebron and then to Gaza. The next night they entered the land ruled by Egypt.

They were safe but without money or food; the son of God was an alien in a foreign land, a refugee. After several harrowing days, they came to Cairo. A Jewish family in the city took them in. They joined a community of Jews who had fled to Egypt to escape Herod's tyranny. The young family remained in Egypt for several years. A good carpenter could always find work in the ancient world, and there Jesus and his family lived until they were summoned home to Nazareth by another angelic dream.

Those who have never been strangers in a strange land will not appreciate what this banishment from their sacred land meant to Mary and Joseph, nor how happy they were as they returned to Nazareth. Although I have never been a refugee, I do know the difficulties of being a parent. I marvel at the courage Mary and Joseph had in rearing the Son of God; they must have been extraordinarily wise parents. We get a glimpse of their wisdom in the only incident recorded of Jesus' youth. After a journey to Jerusalem for the Passover, Jesus' parents gave him such freedom that they did not even miss him until they had spent a day traveling back to Nazareth from Jerusalem. They returned and found him in the Temple—and they took this in their stride. The time was not yet right for Jesus to begin his ministry, so he returned home, learned to be a carpenter, and attended the synagogue school and learned Hebrew and Aramaic. Mary continued to ponder these events in her heart.

When Joseph died, Jesus took charge of the carpentry shop and trained another member of the family to take his place. When Jesus left to begin his ministry, Mary did not stop him. She may not have understood the full meaning of his mission (neither did his disciples), but she watched at the foot of the cross with the other women who accompanied the disciples. She and the beloved disciple heard Jesus' words commending them to one another, and tradition tells us that John and Mary followed Jesus' words. Tradition also has it that she held her son's broken body in her arms after Joseph of Arimathea took Jesus from the cross. She helped the women make preparations for his burial. After Jesus' resurrection, he gathered together his followers and disappeared from them in a blaze of glory. The disciples, together with Mary and the other women who followed him, continued to meet in the upper room in prayer until the Holy Spirit came upon them with tongues of fire.

We have followed Mary beyond Jesus' childhood. If we are to see the full stature of this woman, we need to see how magnificently she lived out her destiny. She was willing to be and to do what God needed. Mary experienced emotional and physical hardship and banishment and never gave up hope. She knew the joy of raising a uniquely gifted child, and she also knew the fear of letting him follow his dangerous vocation. She felt the pain of the sword piercing her heart, yet she did not give way to despair. She was overwhelmed by the ineffable joy of Jesus' resurrection. She joined the disciples in receiving the fullness of the Holy Spirit at Pentecost and supported those who brought a new vision of God to a broken world.

For those of us who wish to have Christ enter our hearts so that we can truly follow him, Mary provides our most complete human model. John Sanford has reminded me that in Greek Orthodox thought Mary is the only human being who has been fully divinized, who realized her full human potential. In his excellent study of Mary, Andrew Greeley describes Mary as

> an extraordinarily intelligent, courageous, devout and charming woman. She could hardly have been anything else. It would seem to me that this solid psychological truth provides us with all the historical information we really need—as pleasant as it would be to have more. I think it more than justifies virtually all the devout reflection that believing Christians have traditionally made on the New Testament data.[8]

Greeley's study is not sentimental romanticism. His description of Mary as the Pieta, Mary holding Jesus in her arms, was the most consoling writing that I encountered as my wife and I ministered to our dying son. Greeley's meditation on this aspect of Mary spoke to me in my human agony when little else touched me: "The acceptance of death does not mean cessation of effort; it means new, more peaceful, better controlled, and more effective effort. Dying, we are reborn."[9]

Any of us who wish to have the Christ born and grow in us can meditate fruitfully on this example, the model of Mary, the mother of Jesus.[10]

4

Joseph the Carpenter

Unless we look carefully at the birth in the stable and the dramatic events that followed it, we may think only of the mother and child. We can even become quite sentimental about the birth in Bethlehem and think of Christmas as a feminine festival, a feast dedicated only to women and children. But where would Mary have been without the sensitivity, the courage and steadfastness, the wisdom and practicality, the support and parenting that Joseph provided both her and Jesus? A lone woman and child could not have survived in the Roman-Jewish society in which they lived. This fact—so obvious to those writing the story of Jesus that they made no note of it—became clear to me when I visited a convent in Bangladesh that took in abandoned babies. In that society a mother cannot earn enough for both herself and her child; she needs a supporting man. In such traditional societies, women without such a male figure are forced to abandon their children, and many children die.

Joseph is a very important character in the Christmas drama, because in that time and culture, Mary simply would not have been able to carry and raise Jesus alone. Most of us, too, seldom stop and reflect on the magnificent person that Joseph must have been. Our appreciation is made even more difficult because the Gospels give us relatively little specific information about him, but we can get a good picture of Joseph as we study the Jewish culture in which he lived.[1] There are numerous pictures of the Madonna and child, but few of Joseph and the child. As I write about Joseph, I have before me a rare exception: a picture of an old wood carving of Joseph and the child found in a rural French church. In his left hand Joseph carries a wooden hammer and in his right arm he is tenderly, affectionately, holding the baby Jesus, his head bent down to touch the child's

head. Who is this man who played such an important role in the protection
and nurturing of the Son of God?

Joseph was a carpenter by trade. He had been trained by his father, who
had moved from Bethlehem to Nazareth because the Greek region around
Sepphores was growing and thriving. In Palestine the upper stories of most
of the stone houses were made of wood, and real skill was needed to make
them secure and keep them in repair. Widespread thievery made it important to have substantial doors and locks, and making these also required
ability and ingenuity. Because iron and metal objects were not common,
workers in wood also made plows and yokes and all the equipment for
threshing and winnowing of grain. Every community of any size needed a
resident carpenter, or civilized life might fall apart. Since most laborers
worked twelve hours a day just to provide for their families, there was no
time to "do-it-yourself." Joseph had an important job, and he did it well.

Joseph came from an old and distinguished family; he counted King
David as one of his ancestors. When the Jews were carried away to captivity in Babylon, the carpenters and smiths were among those taken into
exile. These craftsmen were important, in short supply and highly valued;
they were the technicians of the ancient world. When the Jews returned
from Babylon to their own country, they were ruled first by the Persians,
then the Greeks, and, in Joseph's time, by the Romans. All these rulers
taxed the people heavily. So Joseph's life was hard, and his lineage did not
carry with it much material benefit. He was a survivor who came from a
remnant of survivors. He took his religion seriously and believed that only
through God's grace had his people returned to the Holy Land. He longed
for the time that Israel might again have its own rulers.

Joseph attended the synagogue school in Nazareth where he learned
Hebrew, so he was able to read the sacred scriptures in the original language. In this school he was also taught to follow the religious traditions of
his people. (Such synagogue schools kept alive the Jewish nation as a
people; even today a young man in many branches of Judaism does not
become a full member of the synagogue until he can read the Torah in
Hebrew to his assembled friends and family. In Joseph's day, a Jew who
could not read the Hebrew scripture was hardly considered a real Israelite.) Joseph could speak and write Aramaic, and he knew enough Greek
and Latin to deal with his pagan customers.

Much of Joseph's life was prescribed by religious law. He would not eat
anything unclean. He would not use cooking or eating utensils that were
not properly cleaned. He did not shave or cut his hair short, and he wore
the proper headcovering at the proper times. Hanging on his cloak was a
phylactery with the summary of the law within it. He took care of his
parents as long as they lived. He paid his tithes on all that he earned and
on what grew in his garden. He kept the Sabbath day holy. He looked

forward to Sabbath services at the synagogue and took part in the yearly festivals that reminded him how important it was to receive God's forgiveness and how God had saved his ancestors from bondage in Egypt. He made the annual pilgrimage to the Temple in Jerusalem for Passover. He celebrated each Sabbath eve with the cup of blessing. The whole fabric of his existence was shot through with the thread of the presence of God.

Along with Mary and Elizabeth and Zechariah, he belonged to the Anawim, the poor holy ones. They believed that God was soon going to send a messiah to save God's people and bring all nations to the religion of Israel. They followed the Hebrew law meticulously. Joseph knew his Torah well and believed that God still spoke to ordinary human beings as God had done to Jacob, Moses, and Amos. One did not have to be a priest or scribe to be an instrument of God; even a shepherd, a cultivator of sycamore trees, or a carpenter could be used by God for a holy purpose. God could touch any person with a dream or vision, or by words that spoke in their hearts.

So Joseph, though quite ordinary, was a model of the best of masculine Hebrew religion. He was warm and caring, skilled in his vocation, methodical in his religious practice while still open to new revelation, courageous and stalwart, practical and visionary. Jesus' parable of the prodigal son probably tells something about Joseph as well as it does about the Holy One of Israel. Given this background, we can better understand the conflict that tore Joseph apart when Mary told him about her pregnancy and her angelic visitation; Joseph was too practical to believe Mary's story, but he was such a good man—and so deeply in love—that his doubts about Mary caused him excruciating pain.

In his late twenties Joseph had realized suddenly that Mary, the daughter of Anne, was no longer a child. She was an attractive, devoted, faithful young Jewish woman. Joseph's parents had died some years before, but he had not married because life was difficult, and he did not wish to have a family until he could provide for it properly. He had labored his twelve-hour days to build up his trade and to build a small but adequate home.

He had known Mary's family as long as he could remember; they were faithful in coming to the synagogue and sharing their hopes that the messiah might come and set right the world. He had watched Mary grow from a beautiful child to a vivacious, capable, and deeply religious young woman. They often met at the village fountain, and they had time to talk as they made their trips to Jerusalem. They had chatted when Mary brought a broken broom or rake to be mended by the carpenter. Joseph fell in love; he believed that Mary was the one who would fulfill his life.

When it became apparent that Mary felt as he did, Joseph made the prescribed visit to Mary's parents. He brought fifty shekels, the customary payment when one asked for the hand of a young woman in marriage. He also brought gifts for Mary. His offer of marriage was accepted, and the couple made plans for the formal betrothal. This was a gala occasion; all the friends and relatives were present. The account of the wedding in Cana in the Gospel of John gives us a picture of the festivities that surrounded such an event. For people who live on the ragged edge of poverty, these festivals provided an oasis of plenty in the midst of a tenuous existence. After the betrothal, Mary and Joseph saw each other much more often. Joseph was turning his bachelor's quarters into a home for both of them, and Mary was preparing her trousseau. Both Mary and Joseph were full of the expectation and joy that surround marriage.

Mary's encounter with the angel, and then her realization that the divine messenger had spoken truly, turned their joy into confusion, doubt, and fear. They were faced with a tragic dilemma. They lived in a highly regulated, conventional society. Sexual misconduct was viewed with grave disapproval by the Anawim, and Joseph knew he was not the father of the child. There were Jewish laws—seldom enforced, it is true, but still spelled out—that provided for the stoning of a man and woman caught in adultery. And a betrothed woman who had sexual relations with anyone but her husband was considered an adulterer. Joseph was caught between his religious ideals, his practical human knowledge, and his love for Mary. He was in the position of the priest and Levite who passed the man near death on the road to Jericho; if they tried to help the man and he died in their arms, they would have been excluded forever from their service in the Temple, and yet they knew the importance of loving-kindness.[2] Joseph's decision was not easy.

Joseph loved Mary and he basically trusted her, but this story was just too much for him to believe. Since they were betrothed, and betrothal was tantamount to marriage, their relationship could only be terminated by divorce. He decided to divorce her quietly without announcing the reason for the divorce, and tacitly to take responsibility for fathering the child. Perhaps he thought that his prospective wife was deluded and sick, but he could not go on with one for whom he had no trust. He was preparing to go to the rabbi and write a divorce decree the next day.

That night as he slept he had a strange dream. The atmosphere in the dream seemed vibrant and electric, and then a luminous figure appeared who was both tremendously attractive and frightening—the *mysterium tremendens*, the Holy, an otherworldly being, an angel. Joseph was trembling with holy awe as the figure spoke to him. The angel's stern words burned in his memory: "Joseph, son of David, do not be afraid to take Mary as your wife, for the child conceived in her is from the Holy Spirit. She will bear a son, and you are to name him Jesus, for he will save his people from their sins."[3]

Joseph awoke tingling with a strange wonder, and he realized how wrong he had been. Joseph was a deeply religious man; he had read the scriptures and knew that God sometimes spoke in dreams, and he knew that the Holy One had touched him. His religious knowledge stood him in good stead: His doubt was washed away. He knew now that what Mary said was true. Ashamed of his doubt, he got up, went to Mary, embraced her, and told her that he understood. They made plans for her to move into his house that very week.

If Joseph had not believed that the Holy One of Israel still spoke to human beings and often spoke in dreams, he might have missed the opportunity to father the Son of God. Sometimes our religious experience needs to displace our conventional human wisdom. Saints are those who follow their deepest inner promptings, even when they make no worldly sense.

We know the rest of the story. Once committed, Joseph followed through. When he was called to Bethlehem by imperial decree, he knew he could not leave Mary behind. As a single woman, all alone, she would have received little kindness in Nazareth. Joseph took all possible care of Mary on their arduous journey. He helped with the birth. Amazed, he listened to the shepherds. He made arrangements for the circumcision and the presentation and purification at the Temple. He heard the words of Simeon and Anna. In wonder, he watched the Magi come and go, and then he dreamed again. This time there was no joy in the dream; it was a dream of death and destruction, of horror, bloodshed and murder, a warning dream. The angel showed him the impending slaughter of the infants by Herod. Now sensitive to these spiritual promptings, he roused the child and mother, gathered what food he could find in the total darkness of the night, saddled the donkey, and they fled.

After three terrifying nights of travel, they escaped from Herod's kingdom. The rest of the trip took many weeks. Joseph searched out other Jewish refugee families who helped them on their way. Finally they came to ancient Cairo with a large Jewish community and several synagogues. There Joseph's knowledge of Greek and Latin enabled him to ply his trade. The family lived comfortably, but they longed to return to their own land; they were aliens, refugees with no rights. Several years passed, and then the angelic messenger visited him again as he dreamed. The angel told Joseph that the family could return home safely and directed them back to Nazareth.

Can you picture Joseph in his Nazareth shop, teaching the young Jesus to saw and to plane, to make joints in wood, and to repair anything the villagers brought to them? Try to imagine them going to the synagogue on the Sabbath to listen to the Hebrew readings and to ponder their meaning. As a good father, Joseph helped Jesus to read and write in Hebrew and Aramaic. In addition, Joseph taught Jesus enough Greek and Latin to get along in the Roman world.[4] Every year they went to Jerusalem to the high festivals, although the gospels tell us of only one trip. Then Joseph's understanding wisdom was revealed when Jesus remained behind in the Temple. Joseph was nearly sixty when he died, but Jesus was well prepared to make a living for his mother and the other children. Now it was Jesus who took the family to the synagogue and helped them absorb what it meant to be a true Israelite.

Joseph belonged to a group of Jews who took their religion very seriously. His story reminds us that those who are not trained in some religious tradition are seriously handicapped. Because his religious tradition was one of the world's great religions, it both permeated his entire daily life and opened him to the presence of the Holy. Joseph had indomitable courage, steadfastness, endurance, and hope. His life was disciplined inwardly and outwardly. For Jesus he provided a fine model of masculinity and humanness; he was forgiving, loyal, sensitive, courageous, and caring.

Joseph presents us with an excellent image of fatherhood and masculinity, but he also gives us a clear picture of some of the character traits and qualities that both men and women need if they are to allow the Christ child to grow to maturity within themselves. Joseph shows us how to protect the Christ life in us and set it free and so enable us to realize our divine potential.

For Christ to be born in us and live with us throughout the year, we need the willingness of Mary, but we also need the disciplined steadfastness and sensitive strength of Joseph to support our open willingness. These habits are not as glamorous as the total openness of Mary, but they are just as necessary and important if we are to protect the Christ from our inner Herod and his soldiers.

Like Joseph, we need to be in close touch with the world as it really is. Many religious people let the Christ child die in them because they have no common sense; they live in what they want the world to be rather than what it is. The Christmas story tells us that the world can be hostile to the birth of Christ in our lives. Since the world can be a dangerous place, we need to learn to deal with the threats the world poses to our Christian lives.

Like Joseph, we need to be grounded in a religious tradition and at the same time be sensitive to the moving of the Spirit in prayer, meditation, intuitions, and dreams. We need a regular religious practice of worship and prayer. Then we need the courage to follow our deepest religious wisdom no matter what it costs, even through the dark night of the soul.

Like Joseph, we need the determination to keep up the ordinary humdrum work of our home, shop, or office in order to support, protect, and parent the growing Christ within us. We need discipline. We also need humility; as Joseph was willing to stand in the background, we need to be willing in the same way.

We also need the raw, naked courage Joseph demonstrated when he took Mary on the impossible journey to Bethlehem and when he supported Mary and Jesus during the family's desperate flight to Egypt. The family was never free of terror until they left Herod's kingdom. Even while they were alien refugees, Joseph never gave up hope in what the child Jesus could be.

Joseph was a remarkable human being, a magnificent combination of the best human qualities. He was down to earth and knew how to deal with a difficult world dominated by a foreign power. Joseph, deeply spiritual but also solidly practical, can teach us all. Unless we have our feet on the ground, we seldom can deal creatively with religious experience. Many people who are mentally ill claim marvelous religious experiences, but they cannot do anything with them to make them bear fruit in the world. We need to be as well grounded and practical as Joseph in taking care of the Christ child in us.

Courage is one of conventional Christianity's seldom mentioned foundations. In his book *The Courage to Be*, Paul Tillich describes the courage necessary to our Christian lives. Courage is not an absence of fear but rather an ability to keep on in spite of outer terror or the inner, hopeless dark night of the soul. Those with real courage know that in the end God will bring us through into the kingdom. Mary, Joseph, and Jesus—and most great Christians—are good models of the necessary religious virtue of courage; real religion in a secular world requires it. Christmas vividly displays the importance of openness, love, *and* courage.[5]

5

Blessed Are the Shepherds and the Stable

A dozen cold and hungry shepherds were huddled around a small fire that cast trembling shadows onto the uneven ground. They ranged in age from young children through middle age to white, bearded, seventy-year-old men. Close to the fire one of the younger children lay sleeping. Now and then the child would move convulsively and groan or cry out in the loneliness of his sleep. A lamb came close to another older shepherd and nuzzled his arm. The man reached out his hand and gently stroked the animal's head. He knew what it was like to be a sheep ready for the slaughter. The compassion of shared suffering passed between the shepherd and his sheep. This very closeness to his animals (hardly known in the ancient world) gave him a little consolation and companionship.

The men were grumbling about their hard life as shepherds. The night was even colder than usual, and they were warming their hands over the fire. Suddenly, a great light exploded all around them and out of the light emerged the figure of an angel, a messenger of the Holy One in full power and might. Five of the shepherds fell to the ground quaking with dread; others stood like statues paralyzed in terror. Their fear was perfectly natural. They had been convinced that they were irreligious people and that God was an angry God; they were certain that the powers of heaven had joined the powers of earth and that now they would be utterly destroyed because of their faithlessness, their lawlessness, their rebellion, their helplessness. What could such fearful people expect other than what they had already known? Similarly, the shepherd in so many of us is afraid of the unexpected emergence of the Holy. How could the Divine stand all parts of us? Many men and women deny the existence of the Holy basically to ease their fears of what that reality might be.

The shepherds could hardly believe the angel's words, just as it is often

40

difficult for us to believe them: "Do not be afraid; for see—I am bringing you good news of great joy for all the people: to you is born this day in the city of David a Savior, who is the Messiah, the Lord. This will be a sign for you: you will find a child wrapped in bands of cloth and lying in a manger."[1] Their fear melted away; they got up from the ground, looked at one another, and moved into a circle around the fire. They continued to stare at the angel, and then they saw not only merely one angel but a multitude of angels. The sky was filled with the grandeur and splendor of heaven itself, a glory usually hidden from mortals. The shepherds were lifted out of themselves and they heard the angelic song, with words and music that filled their deepest needs: "Glory to God in the highest heaven, and on earth peace and divine goodwill to human beings."[2] Slowly the shepherds' vision faded; the angels returned to their heavenly realm, and only the stars were shining in the sky.

As the shepherds recovered from their amazement, the deep silence in which they saw and heard the angels' messages was broken. They began to talk excitedly to one another: They found that they all had seen the same vision, heard the same words and music. They were of one mind: They wanted to see this child whose coming was so important. The Holy One of Israel had not rejected them but rather had sent angels to announce to them the birth of a Savior. They were invited to the birth of a Savior who would understand them. They laughed as they talked about a divine being who had been born in a stable—as some of them had been—and whose crib was a manger.

Such a thing seemed absurd to them, but the vision had been so powerful that they had no doubt. A soft wind was rising as they put out their fire and started toward Bethlehem. The road led right by the stable. The light of a lamp filtered through the cracks in the door. Looking at one another, they agreed without words that they should look inside. One of the children ran forward and pulled open the heavy door, revealing a beautiful woman radiant with joy and behind her a tall strong man. In front of the couple they saw the sign that they were looking for—a manger with a newborn baby wrapped in typical Hebrew birth clothes.

A faint glow of the same unearthly light that had shone around the angels surrounded the child and his parents. Now, however, the shepherds were in no way afraid; who would be afraid of a beautiful new baby? Perhaps this is one reason the Holy One came to human beings in this way. The man standing behind the mother and child welcomed the shepherds and asked them to come in from the cold night outside. The leader of the band of shepherds said, "Thank you. Some angels came to us and told us to seek exactly what we have found. When we heard their good news, we came as quickly as we could." Once the ice was broken, the others chimed in with other details of what they had seen and heard. Their words brought joy and confirmation to the weary Mary and Joseph. The shepherds could hardly tear themselves away. One legend tells of a young shepherd who said to the others, "Let us leave a lamb as a present for the baby." They all agreed and an old shepherd laid a sleepy lamb beside the manger-crib.

There were no other guests that night. Mary and Joseph rested in the clean hay with Jesus beside them in his crib. The angels most likely also appeared to some of the good and comfortable men and women who were sleeping in their houses in Bethlehem. Some of them awoke with a chill of fear. Their dreams troubled them, and they thought they ought to get up and look outside; they wondered about the faint light glowing outside in the middle of the night, but their beds were warm, and they needed their rest for the next day's important business. They remained in their beds and were soon unconscious once again. The angels also appeared to the innkeeper and those who were sleeping there. Most of them were sleeping soundly and did not wake up. They moved restlessly in their beds, but no strange dreams aroused them. A few awakened and smiled at their unusual dream of angels and a call to seek out a child who would be a savior. But obviously they would not leave their beds for such an absurd dream. The angels also appeared to the courtiers in Herod's palace, and the next day they made ribald jokes about the treasonous dreams they had shared.[3]

Only the shepherds, then, truly listened to God's angelic messengers. The good news of Christmas, the drama of Christmas, was first revealed to and understood by the poor in spirit, the lost, the forgotten, the anxious, the oppressed. This event dramatizes the words which that baby would speak as an adult again and again to the multitudes who followed him: "Come to me, all you that are weary and are carrying heavy burdens, and I will give you rest."[4] The birth in Bethlehem told these shepherds that the Creator loved them and came to lift their burdens from them. Who were these shepherds and why were they first to find the Christ child?

It is as easy to romanticize the shepherds as it is to romanticize the birth in the stable. These herders of sheep came from the bottom of society. These men were not the independent shepherds of ancient Israel, men like David and Amos. Most of them had lost their land and sheep to moneylenders and large landowners, and were reduced to watching other people's sheep for just barely enough pay to keep body and soul together. They were nearly destitute. Who else would be spending the cold winter nights out under the frigid stars just to stay alive? They are like the swineherd in Jesus' famous story, who went home only because he was starving.[5]

The shepherds were called first because they would be comfortable with a birth in a stable. This was a primitive stable, not a pristine modern dairy. Our Christmas cards deny the reality of the adoration of the shepherds; there was still dung on the floor, swept to one side, and animal saliva had to be wiped from the manger. But the shepherds were perfectly comfortable in this setting. They were not scrubbed pink like those in church pageants or on Christmas cards. These shepherds had not bathed for months. They had been sleeping on the ground. They were dirty, and the human and animal odors would have repelled our delicate Western sense of smell.[6]

These shepherds were outcasts, the dispossessed people of the land. They huddled over little fires in the fields—when they could find enough wood in that semidesert to make a fire. Their condition was far worse than that of most slaves; wise owners took good care of valuable slaves, but no one took care of these forgotten people. The shepherds were helpless and fearful—pawns of rich landholders, of the great Sadducee families of Jerusalem and Bethlehem who cared nothing about them. Over their wine, the wealthy talked of the shepherds as if they were cattle; they ordered these poor people to come or to go, to do this or that. Even worse, when there was no work for them, they were left to beg or starve. Jesus told a story of such workers who waited and waited to be called to labor in a vineyard.[7] The shepherds were sent into the fields because they were not even considered fit to be domestic servants.

The shepherds' position was much like that of the former slaves in Brazil, who were freed not for humanitarian reasons but because they were no longer profitable to keep. Slavery there was only abolished in the 1890s. First, those slaves over the age of sixty were freed, then children under ten, and finally the rest were let go. Families were torn apart, and the tragedy of seven million abandoned Brazilian children began. The shepherds were treated as less than human. The Christmas story then should remind us that oppressed people are as valuable as those who live pleasant lives.

Yet these shepherds were not the animals that some of their masters considered them. They were poor and fearful human beings. They did not like the life they led, did not like the lust and bestiality that sometimes exploded within them. Most of the time they were hungry; they knew the constant, gnawing pain of an angry, empty stomach. They did not like the thefts they committed to get a little more bread, thefts that kept the sentence of slavery or death hanging over their heads.

On top of everything else, their religious leaders laid impossible burdens on the shepherds. They could not possibly keep all the religious law, so they gave up trying to live up to any of it. Their lives were filled with lust and violence, greed and envy, hatred and dishonesty. They did not follow the minutiae of the ritual law; they were unclean, and the scribes and Pharisees had contempt for them. So these poor people felt abandoned not only by their society but also by God and their religion.

Alone under the stars night after night, these burdened people could not hide from themselves; their hearts lay like heavy, leaden balls within them. There was little joy in their lives and a great deal of pain and dread, fear and guilt. Since they were cut off from their religion and forced to scratch out a meager, meaningless existence, they knew the dark and destructive voices within themselves.[8]

For those of us who live in the security and comfort of one of the wealthiest and most powerful nations in human history, it is sometimes difficult to realize that a large percentage of people today live under just such conditions. Even in our prosperous society, we find the same hopelessness among those tormented with mental illness and particularly among the emotionally sick who make up a large percentage of our homeless. In *Our Rag-Bone Hearts*, Elizabeth O'Connor looks into the reasons we ignore and reject these people.[9]

We find the same hopelessness in prisons, among teenage gangs in cities, and in those places ironically called "rest homes." We also find it in war-torn countries all over the world. We "civilized" modern people often are no better than the cruelest people of biblical times.

These poor shepherds are a symbol of those most open to the divine child in Bethlehem. They needed hope in a God who cared. They were naive enough to listen to an angel's words and take them seriously. In addition, these shepherds were *awake, watching, alert, and open*. They immediately set out to find the holy child on that holy night, and they found him. The shepherds at the manger inspire some new beatitudes:

> Blessed are the shepherds, for they give hope to ordinary people like you and me; they tell us no one is excluded.
>
> Blessed are the homeless, wandering, shepherdlike people, for they are free to follow immediately the angel's call.
>
> Blessed are the hungry and thirsty, the unhappy and the unloved, for God has seen their misery and sent divine love bodily into the world at Christmas to assuage their pain and loneliness and give them hope and even joy.
>
> Blessed are those who know themselves so well they are aware of the demons lurking within them, for they are prepared to accept the angel's invitation.
>
> Blessed are the fearful, for the Christ child came to take away their fear and to give them the fullness of heaven's love, now and forever.

Thank God there is a homeless, unloved, frightened shepherd in each of us; this very rejected and despised part of us can lead us to the holy child in Bethlehem who can be our gate to eternal life.

The Stable

We have already noted that the divine Love used history as a parable to confront us humans with our incredible spiritual potential. The Holy One can shatter time with eternity and come among us as a helpless child. "Love divine, all love excelling," wants each of us to know that love wishes to be born not only in Bethlehem in the reign of Caesar Augustus but in every human heart right now. The Holy One wanted us to know that divinity was more acceptable in a stable than in an inn or a palace or even in the comfortable home of one of Bethlehem's solid citizens. The Christ child was born in a stable—a rough, crude, dirty, foul-smelling stable. Slum homes turn the stomachs of some of us; the stable in which the Divine became human was considerably more humble. This particular stable was made so the ass and the ox might survive the winters in Bethlehem—and it was not even comfortable for animals.

Many legends exist about this stable. Often, the legends say, strangers stopped there, coming in out of the cold, dark night to rest in the stable's shelter, and then they slipped away the next day. A runaway slave stopped there one night; he had killed and robbed his brutal master. Another night a drunken soldier passed the night there to sleep off his drunkenness. A prostitute came another night, weary of her labor and of the manifold perversions that sickened her; she rested quietly on the cleaner straw. An abandoned child slept there the night Jesus was born.

A stable was the place the Christ was born. This is a great consolation to me and to most honest human beings, for our souls are often more like this stable—with animal impulses and strange inhabitants—than like a palace or a well-kept inn. If Jesus could have been born in that stable, which housed animals and people like those in the legends, then the Christ can be born in the souls of any of us. None of us can say we are not good enough for love to be born in us, because Jesus was born in a stable where no one was turned out and was visited by poor shepherds who were comfortable there. No one can claim, "I am not good enough," because Christ first came in a stable.

Indeed, Christ is seldom born in people who are complacent and satisfied, in whom everything is snug and in good order. The Christ seems to be born most among men and women whose lives are filled with helplessness and frustration and who cannot seem to make of themselves what they wish. Such people know they are often gripped by strange impulses, and they often feel powerless over those impulses; their weakness and inability to make of their lives what they wish to be gives them humility—and openness to the Christ.

The picture of the Holy Family and the shepherds in the stable suggests still more beatitudes, similar to those that Jesus later shared with his followers on the Galilean hillside:

> Blessed are the stables, for in one of them the Christ child was born.
> Blessed are those whose lives feel like stables and who want to live differently, for in them the Christ can be born.

Blessed are the persecuted and the heavy-laden, those in sorrow, trouble, need, or adversity, for creative love seeks to enter their hearts and be born in them.

We need to swing open the stable doors of our souls and let in the Christ, both newly born and risen from the dead. If we are very quiet long enough, we may hear the gentle knocking of the One who would come in and eat with us. From Matthew to Revelation we find the same message: The Holy One is seeking all of us far more than we seek the Divine. That alone makes us worthy to receive what divine love offers us—the good news of Christmas.

6

The Urchin

There is a legend that Joseph and Mary were not alone when they entered the stable at Bethlehem. Deep in the hay, far in the back of the cave-shed, a young child named Jonathan was hiding. He was a miserable little child, an abandoned boy of seven or eight whom no one wanted or cared about. When he heard the grinding squeal of the opening door and then the voices of the couple who entered the shed, he froze with fear. He was certain the authorities had finally found him and had come to seize him. He was relieved as he heard the couple speak of their desperate situation. The woman was about to have a baby, and the couple had not been able to find any place to stay. They were wanderers, homeless people, just as he was.

The boy felt more at ease when he realized there were others who had no place to stay, who were not welcome anywhere. One of the worst pains of being unwanted is feeling alone in that condition. The inner sense that no one else feels unwanted adds to our loneliness and isolation.

Jonathan's story was tragic but not too different from that of many children of that time or ours. His mother was from Samaria whose people were despised as heretics by the Jews. His father had died shortly after he was born. In order to live, his mother had turned to the only work available to her—prostitution—and she had moved to the anonymous slums of Jerusalem to ply her trade. In a tiny room in the worst part of the city, she scratched out a miserable existence. Men and women who passed her on the street spat at her for being a Samaritan or took advantage of her as a harlot. When they found out who Jonathan was, they jeered at him too. That was just the beginning of the cruelty he was to experience.

Only four months before Jonathan found refuge in the stable in Bethlehem, his mother was taken in the very act of adultery. She was judged by

Hebrew law and stoned. In this way the righteous placated their own guilt by projecting their hatred onto the despised Samaritans. (The law was only invoked when people needed a scapegoat—someone on whom to project their inhumanity.) Jonathan was left all alone to fend for himself.

Putting ourselves back into the mindset of that time is almost impossible unless we have seen pictures of or walked through the slums of Rio or Djakarta, two of the most inhuman places I know. It is hard to believe that human beings can be so abused. Fortunately, in many places, like Europe and the United States, conditions are better than they were in biblical times; the teachings and practice of Jesus of Nazareth have made some differences in how people in these parts of the world view outcasts.

In Jerusalem in those days, people did not take abandoned children into their homes and care for them. After all, this child's mother had been stoned for adultery, and he was a Samaritan. The people of Jerusalem let him live like the dog they thought him to be. During the summer, Jonathan had been able to live by his wits; he was already streetwise. He survived by stealing food and rummaging through garbage. He learned to pick pockets, and when he had a few pennies, he would buy old bread in the cheapest shops. He would munch on it in a deserted hovel or ruined building. Older criminals used him for jobs that only a little boy could get away with. Several times he barely escaped the soldiers who kept order in the teeming city. He knew what would happen to him if he were caught: He would be sold into slavery and never be able to call his life his own again. His was a desperate existence.[1]

As winter storms blustered through the high country around Jerusalem, Jonathan could no longer sleep in the field or in a hidden corner of a deserted ruin. His only protection from the weather was the ragged clothing on his back. He now realized that some of the soldiers and members of the Temple guard recognized him. He could stay no longer in the holy city, so he wandered out into the country toward the village of Bethlehem. All day he had found no scrap of food to steal; he was hungry and brokenhearted, angry, bitter, and filled with hate. It seemed hopeless to go on. No one cared, and his vitality had run out. On the edge of Bethlehem, just as the sun was setting, he found a shed built against a cave in the rock. No one was looking; he squeezed open the door, closed it behind him, and burrowed into the hay in the lowest and most distant part of the cave. He felt about as human as the oxen and donkeys that shared the dirty stable with him. He wept until he fell into a deep sleep.

He was awakened as the stable's newest inhabitants pulled open the stable door. He listened to their talking. He had seen life, and he knew perfectly well, even at his age, what was going on. He heard the man sweeping aside the dung on the stable floor, and he heard the woman's heavy breathing. Then for some reason he did not understand, Jonathan dug himself out of the hay and stepped out toward them. He was expecting to be kicked aside, but instead the man smiled at him with warmth, the first smile directed at him since his mother died.

Jonathan summoned his courage and said, "Is there anything I can do for you?" The man replied, "Yes, thank you. Will you take this bucket to the well at the village square, wash it out, and bring it back full to us?" Twice the boy went, and the second time he returned the man's face was shining with joy as he said, "Come and see." Jonathan followed the man over to a manger filled with clean straw. There he saw a new baby wrapped in swaddling clothes. Quite unconsciously he knelt beside the child and put his hand into the manger; the infant's hand reached up to grasp his.

At that very moment a change took place within Jonathan. The horrible pain and hurt that had been eating away his very soul were mysteriously assuaged and partly washed away. It didn't make sense, but it happened. He felt that someone cared, that he was not all alone anymore. Then his ears were opened, and he heard music such as he had never heard before. He would never forget the words that accompanied the music: "Glory to God in the highest heaven, and on earth peace and divine goodwill to human beings." Suddenly Jonathan felt free and accepted; as the baby held his hand, he poured out his story to this man and woman. They actually listened to him, and he wept healing tears. The man shared bread and cheese with him.

When the shepherds threw open the stable door and were invited in, Jonathan slipped outside and saw the light glowing around the stable-cave. He crept back in, and standing back in the shadows, he watched the shepherds one by one kneel before the baby lying in the straw. He smiled as they presented a lamb to the baby. He especially watched every move the father made; he noticed him beckon to one of the older shepherds and exchange some words with him. Then the shepherd turned, looked at Jonathan, and stepped toward him with an open hand stretched out to him.

At first the residual fear and hatred within Jonathan tempted him to draw back, but his new life helped him stand there and look the man squarely in the face. The old shepherd laid his hand gently on Jonathan's head and spoke softly to him, "Please come with me. We have a very simple hut, but our children are grown and gone, and we would like to have you live with us. Please come. You will be a comfort to my wife." Instinctively the little boy's hand sought out the old man's other hand, and they embraced. They spoke quietly for a few minutes. Jonathan remained close to the shepherd, leaning against his strong leg—he had found what he had always wanted—an *abba* (Aramaic for "daddy") to replace his own. As the shepherds filed out one by one, back to their sheep and fields, Jonathan looked back fondly at the stable where he had been born anew.

Jonathan grew up in that shepherd's household. Even though he was a

Samaritan, his new parents treated him with thoughtfulness and kindness, and he had almost enough to eat. Gradually he began to believe in the world and himself. When he was mature, he left the shepherd's family. He began to buy and sell in the city. He did very well, and he made trips back and forth to many of the cities in Palestine. Whenever he came near Bethlehem, he always stopped to see the shepherd—his *abba*—and his wife. He helped make life more comfortable for them as they grew older. He was always open to the downtrodden, the needy, and the depressed. On one trip to Jericho he found a man who had been robbed and lay half dead. He dressed the man's wounds and placed him on his donkey. When they arrived at Jericho, he took him to an inn and cared for the man all night. When he left, he gave the host two silver coins to care for the beaten man; he would make up the difference when he returned.

Many similar legends tell of this stranger in the cave. Once, after I told the story of Jonathan, a woman spoke up and added another legend from a recording she had for many years: It told of a little boy like Jonathan, who lived at the inn, but he had been so abused and frightened that he could not speak. He thought he had no tongue. A group of drunken men seized the lad and made him dance on the table as they ridiculed him. Once the inn had closed, the child wandered out into the night; it was so quiet he could hear the stars sing and the wind rustling through the grass. He thought, *Oh, they have no tongues, either, but they can sing.*

That night he went into the stable where he usually slept, and he saw a little baby in a manger. He went up to the manger, and the little baby reached for his hand and touched him. It was as if love had touched him, and he opened his mouth and sang a lovely lullaby as his gift to the baby Jesus. Another version of the story, presented by Caryl Porter in her sensitive book *To Make All Things New*,[2] tells of a frightened and abused little girl who came into the stable and was touched by the holy child. In her poetic prose, Porter describes how this experience eventually changed the life of the woman that child became.

All these stories tell the same message about the Creator's entrance into creation: No one is excluded, utterly no one. When we touch the Holy, our souls and minds and even our bodies can be healed. In a letter, Jung wrote:

> You are right. The main interest of my work is not concerned with the treatment of neuroses but rather with the approach to the numinous. But the fact is that the approach to the numinous experiences is the real therapy and inasmuch as you attain to the numinous experiences you are released from the curse of pathology.[3]

"Pathology" is the medical word for sickness, while "numinous" is the word Jung uses for the holy. One of the easiest ways of meeting the transforming, holy love of the Creator is at the stable in Bethlehem. Many have stopped before that manger and felt the touch of the infant's hand, and through it the power of the Creator, the very power that spun out our universe. For some the infant conveys new life, while for others it is primarily the luminous figure of the risen Christ who conveys this life. Incarnation and resurrection are two parts of one caring Divinity.

Sometimes human caring can be a channel for divine love; this is beautifully illustrated by a story that Aniela Jaffé has told about Jung. A little girl was brought to Jung's office. She could not speak, but she did not seem to suffer from any neurological or physical illness. She had visited many doctors. She spent an hour with Jung and came out speaking. When asked what he had done, he replied, "Oh, I put her on my lap and sang to her."[4]

Most of us appear to outside observers to be adults capable of dealing with the world; however, a great number of us carry within us a hurt and damaged child that never grew up. This child is still very real, very present: neither space nor time exists in the spiritual world. Therefore, we can bring this hurt and fearful part of ourselves to the healing, restoring, caring child-Creator. The Holy One so loved the world that the divine child came in Bethlehem for us; and we can sometimes feel healing as we allow this reality to enter our deepest and most painful memories. So this cringing, frightened child living in all of us actually can lead us to healing and salvation.

Human transformation is genuinely possible when people live within the reality of the miracle of Christmas throughout the year. Since true stories of such transformation can make this possibility more real, I will end the chapter by sharing one of my favorites.

In the year 1878 in Manchester, England, a young Catholic man of nineteen was refused admission to study for the priesthood of the Roman Catholic Church. This was one failure. He then failed in the study of medicine, then in the armed services, and after that his mother died. He was given a copy of Thomas DeQuincey's *Confessions of an English Opium-Eater*, and he became an opium addict. He drifted into London and survived on the streets of the slums selling matches. Under the gaslight of Charing Cross, on dirty scraps of paper, he wrote several poems and an essay on paganism. He sent them in a dirty envelope to Wilfred Meynell, the editor and publisher of *Merry England,* the leading Catholic magazine in England. In cleaning out his desk sometime later, Meynell opened the envelope and found the signs of literary ability on the messy pages. He published one of the poems, "The Passion of Mary," though he could find no trace of the author.

One day a knock came on the door of the Meynell home. A man in rags and disintegrating shoes stood before the publisher. He said, "I am the man who wrote the poem, 'The Passion of Mary.'" The Meynells took the young man into their home in spite of his record of failures. He gave up opium. They arranged for him to stay in a Catholic priory. That young man was Francis Thompson, the author of one of the greatest religious poems in the English language, "The Hound of Heaven."

What was the secret of the Meynells' healing power? They lived the spirit of Christmas in their hearts and actions throughout the year. They had the courage to take the destitute young man into their home; they were acting with the same kind of hope our divine Creator had on entering creation. It is tragic if the spirit of the holy birth motivates us only for a few days in December. But how can we continue to feel as we did as children at Christmas? How can we look out into our broken world with hope and confidence, with the belief that in the end love is the ultimate reality, and then act toward others as if this were true? The story itself gives us many hints. John Shea offers suggestions about how we can accomplish this in his provocative new book, *Starlight: Beholding the Christmas Miracle All Year Long.*[5]

7

The Innkeeper

The Holy One of Israel sought to reach out to humankind by being born as a human child, but those who were chosen to bring forth this child and nurture him could not even find a room in a human dwelling where the birth could take place. The Holy One had come among his chosen people, and even these chosen ones did not receive their divine protector. The divine heart of reality saw the couple turn from the open doorway and wander dejectedly down the hill as they looked for the stable door. They could travel no farther; they had to find a place to stop—the baby was about to be born. Sadly, this was not the only time humans have closed the entrance of their hearts to the divine lover.

The Old Testament tells stories of men and women opening their lives to the Holy One just a bit and then closing them again. Divine love sought us out for centuries and came among us as one of us, as Jesus of Nazareth, as a baby in a manger. Yet, for the two thousand years that followed this event, much of our world has treated the Christ as the innkeeper treated Mary, Joseph, and the baby in Mary's womb.

Seldom have most of us recognized the Christ when he came to us, and even more seldom have we truly tried to follow his way of unconditional love. Christ has been turned away from many doorways. Nations have closed their portals and gone on with power politics as usual. Schools, industries, and even churches have decided that the person and way of the risen One are irrelevant to the workaday world. Most of us have at times closed down the gate to the Christ and gone our disastrous, selfish ways. We can better understand how difficult it is to let the Christ into our lives when we try to understand that first rejection—when we learn something about the innkeeper.

Most of us have been given the wrong picture of the "inn" and the

"innkeeper." Viewing the innkeeper as a cruel and thoughtless man simply looking for financial gain, a man who laughed at the misery of the
young couple, is not correct. The inn was not a penny-pinching commercial establishment from which these poor travelers were brusquely turned
away.

Some modern versions of the New Testament do not translate the
Greek word as "inn" at all. Joseph and Mary were not turned away from
an ordinary hotel; such places were only found on the great trade routes,
and Bethlehem was not on any major trade route. The Greek word translated "inn" in so many old versions of the Christmas story is the same word
used for the upper room in the story of the last supper. The word really
means "guest chamber."[1]

In the days of an independent Palestine, some wealthy and charitable
families around Jerusalem added one or several large rooms to their personal homes. The rooms were built not for commercial gain but for kind,
thoughtful hospitality. Because the Jews had been wanderers for years
after their escape from Egypt, hospitality was considered a great virtue in
Hebrew society. Jews throughout the Roman Empire longed to come to
Jerusalem. The owners of the great houses then considered it a religious
privilege to help pilgrims who came to the holy city, and other travelers
also were welcome. Joseph and Mary were turned away from a guest house
built for such pious, generous reasons. This lodging was very different from
the greedy host in Bethel who had demanded such a high fee. This fact
heightens the irony and tragedy of their rejection. (Even more sadly and
ironically, later in his life Jesus was opposed by the very group of wealthy
and religiously proper people who had built these lodgings.)

Tradition has given the name of Nathan to the owner of these guest
chambers. His father came from an old and wealthy family that owned
thousands of acres of land and tens of thousands of sheep and goats. His
father, a deeply religious man, realized that, since the Roman peace, Jews
were coming from all over the ancient world to Jerusalem and they needed
a place to stay when they came. Bethlehem, as the home of David, was also
a sacred town. It was near Jerusalem, so it was a very appropriate place for
a great house. On one side of his large home, Nathan's father had built
several large, comfortable rooms that could house a large family, as well as
several smaller, individual rooms. This was not a commercial venture; Nathan's father had increased the family holdings and money was a matter of
no concern.

In addition, the family retained many servants and slaves to care for the
family as well as the guests' rooms. In a very real sense, the travelers were
the guests of the family when they entered Nathan's father's door. If they
made a gift in gratitude, it was given to the Temple. It was a matter of
common knowledge that these rooms were open to any who needed them.

Although the rooms were most often filled at Passover, some people could be found there at any time. These rooms had been a great boon to many travelers.

When his father died, Nathan, the only male child, became master of the family properties. He had been raised in the strict tradition of the priestly Sadducees. He had been well educated, was on friendly terms with the Roman leaders, and had traveled to Rome; he was a cultured gentleman. He had a fine wife, to whom he was deeply devoted, and three lovely children. He was an excellent father and a steadfast friend. He was religious in an external way; he was meticulous in giving his tithes, and he went regularly to the local synagogue and attended all the major rituals in the Temple. He took good care of his servants and slaves and did many good works. His favorite charity was maintaining the guest lodging that his father had built. He enjoyed mixing with his guests; he was always gracious. He had a keen sense of humor and told marvelous stories. This was the man who turned away the couple who were about to give birth to the Son of God.

On that fateful night, Bethlehem, because of the census, was packed with people from all over Palestine. (The family of David was a large one.) Nathan's guest rooms were filled to the brim. He was congratulating himself that he had kept these guest quarters ready for this unexpected influx of people; he was pleased with his father's forethought in building these rooms, and he was proud of the opportunity it gave him for hospitable charity. Just then there was a knock on the door. Nathan went over and opened the door himself. Behind him a fire blazed on the hearth. Before him in the dark stood a travel-worn young man, his clothes splattered with mud. In the deeper shadows behind the young man, Nathan could see a young woman on a donkey; her face revealed anxiety and distress. The young man spoke directly, "Is there any room? My wife is due to deliver her child at any moment." Nathan looked at the young man and the woman, and shaking his head sadly, he said, "No, I am very sorry, but we filled up the last suitable place just a few minutes ago. There is no room. However, there is a stable just down the hill where you can rest for the night."

The truth of the matter was that Nathan hated to displease anyone. Some of his guests could have been moved closer together to make room for this couple, but Nathan didn't want to offend them. It was easier for him to turn away the young man and woman than to rearrange the cordial, cultured people who were already comfortably settled in his lodging. If Nathan had thought these people were important, he probably would have made the effort to rearrange the guest quarters, but this couple was only a common artisan and his wife. In addition, Nathan also realized that having a baby in the house might cause considerable commotion and disturb him and his guests. The couple could get along in the stable, and from the looks of them, they were not used to much better. At least the stable had clean straw. If he had been a little kinder, he would have shown them the way to the stable or sent a slave down with them. If he had been a little more spiritually sensitive, he might have detected the faint radiance that surrounded the woman—but Nathan was not used to looking for the spiritual in the ordinary world.

What was the matter? Why did he not perceive who these people were who had come to his door? Why was his lodging house not the birthplace of the Messiah? There were many reasons.

Probably the most significant blind spot was that he had limited expectations of what God could do. It never occurred to him that God might use him in any special way. He did not believe that anything new or exciting could happen to him. He believed everything essential to religious belief and practice had been written down in the sacred book of his people, the sacred Scripture. He had studied the Jewish law and knew it well. He could not imagine that the Holy One of Israel would demean himself to the point of stepping down into the lives of men and women. He was not watching or expecting anything new. When we are not expectant, are not looking for something new, we seldom find anything new. Prospectors who are not looking for gold can walk right past it. Science that is not looking for new truth usually dies. To find, we need to have some idea of what we are looking for.

Nathan had everything he wanted, and he was not expecting anything new or better. His life was comfortable and pleasant. We have already noted what Jesus stated again and again: the uncomfortable and the searching, the unsatisfied and the empty are the ones most likely to seek and find new life.

Because of his complacency, Nathan had paid no attention to recurrent dreams that awakened him from his slumber, dreams of great opportunities coming to him, of doors opening and revealing a great light, or just dreams about a wide-open door. He was aware that dreams had been very important to the patriarchs, the founders of Israel. But since he knew he was no patriarch or prophet, and he assumed the Holy One would not bother with him, he ignored these strange, recurrent dreams. In addition, Nathan had tremendous responsibilities. He was very busy running his huge estate; he took little time for reflection or quiet or private prayer. He was just too busy to become quiet and mull over the recurrent image of the great, luminous open door. Nathan lived in only one dimension, and he was quite happy and well satisfied.

The couple departed. Nathan locked the large carved door of the guest house, and he turned his attention to his present guests, making sure they were properly cared for. Then he went to bed. During the night he was awakened by the strains of strange, magnificent music, and he saw a bright light shining through his bedroom window. Again, since he was not expecting anything, he dismissed the music as a dream caused by the excellent wine he had consumed at supper. He assumed the light was a flash of winter lightning or a bonfire built by village revelers.

The next morning, three of Nathan's shepherds brought milk from his flocks for his guests. He listened patiently as they excitedly told him about their vision of angels and about the heavenly music and consoling angelic words they had heard. In addition, they said they had found a newborn child just as the angels had described him. Nathan smiled indulgently and thanked God that his superior education and good practical sense kept him from being taken in by such superstition. He told the shepherds he was happy for them, but when they asked him to come with them and see the child, Nathan replied he was far too busy with more important matters. So he missed seeing the Christ child. The stable and the holy family would have welcomed him, just as they welcomed the shepherds, had he made the effort.

Thirty years later Nathan was on business in Capernaum where a great prophet and healer was speaking to large crowds and healing all sorts of sicknesses. His friends told him he really should take the time to go, see, and hear this man, but Nathan replied to them, "My wife and children are in good health. The Temple and the synagogue are good enough for me. I have all the religion I need. You know how busy I am getting supplies for the guest house. I am very busy; I just don't have time."

A few years after that, four of his guests—who were present for the Passover—told Nathan of the excitement in Jerusalem. A great prophet had been crucified, but his followers claimed he had been raised from the dead. Now his followers, ordinary peasants and fishermen, were speaking with power and also healing the sick. Nathan listened politely; he was always polite. But he thought to himself, *Why do people accept such ludicrous ideas? These men seem to be reasonable people.* So Nathan missed the Christ, who came so close to him three times. Many of us do the same; the Holy One tries to enter our lives, but we politely, ever so politely, show him the stable down the hill.

It is not easy to stay alert for the presence of the risen Christ when he seeks to come into our lives. We need to be more than nice, educated, generous, cultured people to hear the knock on the doorways of our souls. Nathan had all these virtues, yet he failed to see who was at his door. Sometimes only desperation can sharpen a person's inner eye to see the One who can deliver humans from anguish and even death; other people are led to see this deliverer just because they are hungry and seeking for more of life than they already have. The basic purpose of the fellowship of Jesus' followers is to provide for the spiritual growth of both kinds of people, the desperate and the seeking. Such fellowship enables all of us to find the transformation and healing that come as we are touched by the holy. We need companionship in which to share our deepest spiritual experiences if we are to integrate them into the fabric of our lives.

In a true Christian fellowship we learn to listen to one another and to share our spiritual experiences. We read, study, and inwardly digest the Bible and its crowning glory, the New Testament. We share those insights that come to us as we meditate on the revelation of the Holy One's love for us. We listen to one another and try to share the same kind of love that Jesus demonstrated for us in his life and stories and teaching. We learn to be quiet and learn that the same God who came to Joseph in his dreams may speak to us in our dreams or in a still, small voice in the quiet of the night.

Within this fellowship we discover, as we listen to others, that the light and presence of the Divine are to be found even in the most unlikely people. We can learn from poor people like the shepherds. Reaching out to the most destitute, we often receive much more than we have given. We never know in what guise the Christ child will come to us; we need to be expectantly watching and spiritually sensitive if we are to welcome the Holy One in whatever way the Divine wishes to enter our souls. We need fellowship with other seekers to keep us honest with ourselves and on our way to human fulfillment. The Church of the Saviour in Washington, D.C., takes people to places all over the world where poverty is rampant. Most visitors find they are ministered to more than they minister: those whose faith has overcome their limited living conditions give many people a new vision of what Christian service can be.[2]

8

A Third Road
to Bethlehem

Few parts of the Christmas story have stirred Christian interest and imagination more than the arrival of the Magi. In the Roman catacombs are paintings, dating from as early as the second century A.D., of the Magi coming and giving their gifts to the Christ child. Also from the same time period, Christian writings about the Magi enlarge on the gospel story. Throughout the Christian era, a favorite subject for Christian mosaics and paintings has been the homage paid to the infant Jesus by these princely, priestly Wise Men of the East. The same interest continues today. Last year a Utah museum added a vivid painting of the Magi to its permanent collection.

Interestingly, the portrayal of the shepherds' visit became popular in Christian art and thought only in relatively recent years as the mission of Christ to the poor and dispossessed has become more and more clear. Many followers of Christ have come to regard God's concern for men and women as being similar to that of a shepherd to sheep. These followers have felt called to live among the broken and forgotten and bring the Christ child to them.

Common tradition has settled on the number of Magi as three, each bringing a quite different gift. Tradition in the West has given them the names "Balthasar," "Melchior," and "Gaspar," and each is seen as representing one of the races of humankind; this tradition was firmly established by the eighth century.

Who were these mysterious Magi? Ancient historians told of priestly leaders from Media and Persia who were scientists, astronomers, astrologers, and interpreters of dreams and visions. They were the wise men of the time both in secular and religious matters. In his monumental book,

Shamanism: Archaic Techniques of Ecstasy, Mircea Eliade describes people of all cultures who were open to the spiritual world, and the Magi were exactly the kind of people whom Eliade describes. The Magi of the Christmas story had a vision of a monarch who would bring peace to the world. Since Judaism had spread throughout much of the Near Eastern world, they would not have been surprised to find that this leader might be king of the jews. The Magi were seekers, not satisfied with the world as they knew it; they hoped this leader would be someone who could make the world better. After their vision and the appearance of a strange star, they decided to set out to find this new king. They made their plans, gathered together a caravan, and started on the long journey to Judea. They were not just pious visionaries; they were willing to wager their money and their energy (and perhaps their lives) to seek out this king of peace.[1]

None of the roads to Bethlehem were easy to travel, as we saw when we meditated on the journey of Mary and Joseph. And the Magi, unlike the shepherds, had to travel a long road; they had to face adversity to reach their goal. The shepherds, of course, also knew adversity, and it had prepared them to accept the angel's message. But once the angel came to them and they got over their fright, the shepherds simply had to cross the field to find the Christ child. (Likewise, millions of slaves and day laborers, men and women like the shepherds, flocked into the new Christian fellowship; a god born in a stable spoke directly to them.) The Magi had the longest and most difficult journey to Bethlehem. Until we reflect on their journey, we are likely to have a romantic and sentimental picture of their pilgrimage. They were not riding on richly caparisoned horses, camels, or elephants. They were not arrayed in spotless cloaks of purple velvet or robes of crimson damask. If they had any crowns or silk turbans decked with jewels, these would have been carefully hidden away in the saddlebags. They were not dressed as they would have dressed for a short journey from their palaces to some nearby mountain villages. This was an enormous voyage.

We have forgotten what travel was in those days. We children of the twentieth century, who can get onto a plane in New York after breakfast and arrive ready for a formal lunch in Los Angeles, have never known what caravan travel was. We can hardly imagine the danger, the personal sacrifice, the hardship of a desert journey under the best of conditions. Most caravans only left in the spring or summer, and these Magi came in the dead of winter when most caravan lodgings were closed and some routes had been abandoned. Their trip took several months and covered a thousand miles. Few writers have captured the reality of the Magi's journey better than T. S. Eliot:

A cold coming we had of it,
Just the worst time of the year
For a journey, and such a long journey:
The ways deep and the weather sharp,
The very dead of winter.
And the camels galled, sore-footed, refractory,
Lying down in the melting snow.
There were times we regretted
The summer palaces on slopes, the terraces,
And the silken girls bringing sherbet.
Then the camel men cursing and grumbling
And running away, and wanting their liquor and women,
And the night-fires going out, and the lack of shelter
And the cities hostile and the towns unfriendly
And the villages dirty and charging high prices:
A hard time we had of it.
At the end we preferred to travel all night,
Sleeping in snatches,
With the voices singing in our ears, saying
That this was all folly.[2]

At home these three Magi had all the comforts of princely living, but
something was missing; they were restless and unsatisfied. Then they were
given a common vision of life with a center, of meaning, and of a new kind
of deity whose essence was peace and love. They were willing to risk
everything to find the reality their vision promised. Most people could not
see the star they followed, and few knew the heavens as well as these
Magi. They were like Polynesians who set out across uncharted oceans to
find new lands by following the stars and then returned home by the stars
to bring their families and animals, their plants and crafts, to settle the
fertile islands.

The Magi knew the journey was perilous, and they could not be sure
they would find their king of peace. They knew the dangers of deserts and
mountain passes, as well as of the bandits who preyed on travelers. They
knew all this before starting, and yet their vision was worth the gamble.
The Magi were spiritual adventurers and carried, hidden in their mud-
stained saddlebags, expensive treasures fit for a king: gold from the ancient
mines of Persia, frankincense from the balsam trees of Arabia, and precious myrrh from rare trees of the East. They were prepared to pay homage to this newborn king. They arrived after Jesus had been circumcised
and presented in the Temple and after Mary's purification. Their journey
took longer than even they had expected.

The Magi wanted something more than they already had, something
their vision promised; they had the courage to wager their lives and com-

fort, their pleasure and reputation, and to start out under the gray winter skies. At night a star led them. The gifts they brought were of great value, but their greatest gift was the journey itself, the courage that prompted it, and their faith in their vision; their very coming was the highest homage they could pay. The Magi were seekers after the best that heaven and earth could give, so they set out against insuperable odds. They often thought of turning back. A dark voice within them grumbled, rebelled, and scorned them. They often remembered the laughter of the other Magi back home, who mocked them and made fun of their venture. Sometimes they lost sight of their star. The Magi fought an inner battle, and also fought the wind and the sand, the snow and the cold, the bandits, and the barren desert.

How did they make it through? They had one another and a common quest. When one was discouraged, the others listened and offered encouragement. When another thought of returning, he was told he was needed, or he was reminded of the vision they all had and of the wonder they were seeking.

The camaraderie of the Magi is a key element of the story. Few people can make such a journey alone; the journey toward the center, toward wholeness, toward Divinity is seldom easy. We need one another. Most religions have temples and companions to guide us on our way and to help us bear our burdens. The Spanish philosopher Unamuno wrote that the chief sanctity of a temple is that it is a place where men and women can come and weep together. We also need a place where we can rejoice and sing together. One of the great values of a church is the companionship of like-minded people following the same star, the Risen One, the divine child in Bethlehem. Most of us need faithful companions if we are to find our destination.

Henry Van Dyke wrote of Artaban, a fourth magus, who failed to meet the other three as they started out. On the way he found a sick and dying Hebrew man. He nursed the dying man, and the man recovered. The wise man's grateful patient shared with him the prophecy of the birth of the Messiah in Bethlehem. The wise man then set out alone, but his act of mercy had so delayed him that he arrived in Bethlehem after Mary, Joseph, and Jesus had fled. A Hebrew woman then took him into her humble home. When the soldiers of Herod descended on the village, Artaban saved her young child by bribing a soldier with a jewel intended as a gift for the Christ child. He continued his search all over the ancient world and finally came to Jerusalem at the Passover thirty-three years later. He might have seen Jesus being led to crucifixion, but with his last gift, a great pearl, he ransomed a woman being dragged away to be sold as a slave. During the Good Friday earthquake, the fourth magus was struck by a falling roof tile. As he died, the woman he had saved heard him say, "Not so, my Lord, for when saw I thee hungry and fed thee? or thirsty and gave thee drink?" Even though he never saw the living Jesus with his physical eyes, he carried the divine child in his heart. He lived the Christ life by caring for those who needed him.[3]

To appreciate fully the journey of the Magi then, we need a more accurate picture of these men and their caravan as they entered Judea. They were not polished and fresh. Their faces were burned by the wind and the sand of the desert. Their turbans were frayed, and their silver trappings were tarnished and dull. They slumped in their saddles from sheer exhaustion. The camels were dirty and presented a sorry spectacle. Yet the Magi had a vision, and the courage to make the journey and find the infant Messiah.

It hardly seems fair they had to come so far, through so many deserts, to ford so many rivers, to cross so many mountains in countries where oases were seldom encountered. Yet their gifts would have meant little had they only crossed the street of their village and offered their gifts with a flourish. Some of us are fated to find the Christ child only after such a journey. Worldly wisdom needs to make sacrifices to find the new Divinity that dared to be born as a child. Most wise ones need to make quite a trek if they are to find abiding meaning. Simple folk can usually find their ridiculous Holy One by crossing a field like shepherds; they bring their poverty, humility, their simple openness. But knowledge and wisdom that do not seek something beyond what they already possess often end in despair. People who believe they have the final truth often are led into ugly dead-end streets or lost in the desert.

Are not most of us more like the Magi than we are like Mary and Joseph and the shepherds? The story of the Magi tells me that even the wise and doubting, the well-informed and intelligent, can find the treasure of the Christ child. The comfortable and well-educated can find the baby in Bethlehem; however, they usually have a long journey to make.

For most of us this is an inner journey, a journey like that described by John Bunyan in *Pilgrim's Progress*. Such a spiritual journey is not made easier by modern transportation. Our inner star leads us on our long journey to the inner light of the divine lover and takes us through the shadowy parts of ourselves. It leads through dry deserts, across great mountains and unfordable rivers, through the great abyss, through swamps and many tempters and false destinations. Many times we will wish to give up the venture; seeking to open our souls to the Christ child means risks, sacrifice, and wagers on evidence our heads think are insufficient. Jesus himself told his followers that the way to eternal life was narrow and steep.

Without our companions on the way, we might despair of the barren dryness and the impenetrable swamps and just give up. However, if some of our companions have been through this country before, they know there are resting places not far ahead. Few people can make such a journey alone; even the shepherds needed to be encouraged by companions. Those who claim that finding and bearing the Christ child are easy may be on the wrong freeway. But when we finally see the lights of Bethlehem and see our star still shining there, after we have passed the last peaks and desert sands, then we see him lying there before us. We kneel and the sound of angelic music, the heavenly choir, breaks in on us, and we see the magnificent splendor, the ineffable glory of the Creator as a baby in a crib. Then we are embraced by divine love; we understand how little we have offered by our journey.

The harbor is a million times worth the voyage. The light of the divine presence burns out the dross in us, renews and refills us, and gives us hope, love, faith, and joy. We are filled with something more than we ever dreamed we could have. We even tend to forget the swamps and the endless dry sand of the journey and rejoice that we were given the star (and each of us *has* been given a star to lead us). If we had never made the journey, we would have nothing, would still be lost in the desert.

The importance of indomitable persistence is magnificently portrayed by Goethe in *Faust* and sung by the heavenly choir in Mahler's Eighth Symphony based on Goethe's play. Mephistopheles has come to take Faust's soul off to hell as he is dying. At that moment, a troupe of angels— led by Gretchen, whom Faust betrayed, Mary Magdalene, and the woman at the well—swoop down and carry Faust off to heaven as the choir sings:

> Those whose seeking never ceases
> Are ours for their redeeming.[4]

It is just such persistence that the Magi embody.

The Magi would have been far wiser to have followed their vision and their star without a stop in Jerusalem. But they saw the walls and towers of the great city of the Jews and thought the people living in the center of Jewish life would know about the new religious leader they sought. Politically the Magi were naive; before they started asking about a new king of the Jews, they should have discovered the political climate in Judea and Jerusalem. Anyone could have told them that the city was filled with Herod's spies and that Herod was paranoid about the possibility of any threat to his power or his dynasty.

Herod was startled and frightened when his informers reported three strangers asking about a new Jewish king. Knowing of Herod's violent rage, the leaders of the city trembled as well. Herod immediately summoned the chief leaders of the people, both the priests and the scribes, to learn of any prophecies about where the messiah would be born. They searched the scriptures diligently and found two references to Bethlehem in Judea as the birthplace of the messiah. The scholars combined the passages and told Herod the scriptures stated: "And you, Bethlehem, in the land of Judah, are by no means least among the rulers of Judah; for from you shall come a ruler who is to shepherd my people Israel."[5] Herod then sent several secret messengers to invite the Magi to visit his palace.

More astute religiously than politically, the Magi accepted Herod's cordial-sounding invitation. Herod seemed sincere, gracious, and quite wise; he had available the information the Magi desired, and he was willing to share it. For reasons of his own, Herod inquired about the exact time the star appeared, and then he sent the Magi off to find the child. In his warmest manner he begged them to return and report to him; he said he wanted to come and pay homage to the child himself. The Magi did not detect his deception, and they hurried off to find the child.

Herod's information was quite unnecessary, as the star they had followed so long rose before them and stopped right over the house in which they found the child and Mary and Joseph. Their joy was boundless; their journey had not been in vain. They knew they had found the One they sought. They knelt before the child to give homage and admiration. Their servants brought out their treasure chest; one presented a pouch filled with gold coins, another a jeweled casket of frankincense, and the third an alabaster jar of myrrh. The gifts were worthy of a king.

It was late at night before they lay down in the guest house. They were thinking how grateful Herod would be for their news. But Melchior's sleep was disturbed by a nightmare of Herod plunging a sword into the holy child. He awakened the others, told them his dream, and all three were horrified as they realized their stupidity. Now they realized they had been followed. In the dead of night their servants saddled their animals, and they all started home through the trackless desert where no one would find them. Like all religious seekers, they needed to be as gentle as doves and as wise as serpents.

The Magi's visit and the gifts they brought added a new dimension to Mary's ponderings. Mary and Joseph began to realize that the child entrusted to their care was more than a messiah for Israel. Their child had worldwide importance as the prophets of Israel had proclaimed, the Holy One of Israel was a universal deity, one for all nations and people; the life and ministry and words of Jesus were meant for all humankind. Mary lived long enough to see the ministry of Jesus reach into all parts of the Roman world. The visit of the Magi was the first evidence, the tip of the iceberg, of the limitless significance of this Jewish messiah, the Son of God.

Herod waited for several days for the Magi's return, and then he realized he had been tricked. Rage possessed him. If he did not know which child in Bethlehem to slay, he would slay them all. He sent his soldiers out on their despicable mission. Since a messiah was a king, a rival, the Messiah must be destroyed. The Romans, years later, would want a messiah from Judea no more than Herod had; nailed above the head of the crucified Jesus was this sarcastic inscription: THE KING OF THE JEWS.

T. S. Eliot concludes his poem "Journey of the Magi" by revealing how much Jesus' birth and death are linked. Christmas and Easter are parts of the same story. One of the Magi speaks:

> All this was a long time ago, I remember,
> And I would do it again, but set down
> This set down
> This: were we led all that way for
> Birth or Death? There was a Birth, certainly,
> We had evidence and no doubt I had seen birth and death,
> But had thought they were different; this Birth was
> Hard and bitter agony for us, like Death, our death.
> We returned to our places, these Kingdoms,
> But no longer at ease here, in the old dispensation,
> With an alien people clutching their gods.
> I should be glad of another death.[6]

I wonder if news of the slaughter of the children and of the death and resurrection of Jesus ever reached the Magi in their palaces far to the East.

9

The Herod
in Us All

Herod lay brooding in the lavish private chambers of his magnificent palace. Herod the Great, as people already had begun to call him, was old and sick and frightened; he feared his hold on power was loosening. Gaining and keeping this power had been no easy task even in better times. His father had gradually acquired and consolidated power; he had been made the first Roman procurator of Judea. Herod's own greater success had been a miracle of political vision and diplomatic craft. After Julius Caesar's assassination, chaos had ensued, but Herod had been able to pick the winning side in the civil war, and he threw all his power to Augustus and Agrippa. He was rewarded with the title of king and had ultimate power in Judea for forty years. Now, however, he was old, losing his physical strength. He clung to his power and his kingship as a drowning man grasps for a plank.

He had just been informed by his spies that three strange people were in Jerusalem asking treasonous questions. They were asking about the birth of a new king of the Jews. Herod knew perfectly well there had been no births in his royal family, nor were any expected. He wondered if this could be an omen that foretold the rise of another royal line that might question his rule. Herod had given his life, his very soul, to establish his dynasty; he was determined to do all in his power to maintain his family's rule. The very thought of losing power was more than Herod could bear. He decided to investigate immediately and to invite the three men to visit him. However, he must be prepared; he summoned the chief priests and the scribes. These men had supported him as he rose to power. They wanted no trouble with Rome that might disturb their privileged position. They worked together and found a scriptural passage about the messiah that would satisfy the king.

Armed with this information, Herod sent a cordial and friendly messenger to invite the three men to his palace. Being a cultivated man, used to wealth and nobility and acquainted with most of the important people in the empire, Herod knew gentility when he saw it. When these three entered, he knew immediately he was dealing with lords of the East. These princely Magi were from Persia, a country so powerful that even Rome did not try to attack it. Even though the dirt of the road stained their apparel, Herod perceived the wealth of their clothes—these, and their manners were impeccable. In his most genial manner Herod asked of their journey and its object. Without a trace of guile they told their whole story. Herod showed great pleasure and told them he just happened to know where they might find the one they were seeking; then he inquired carefully the time their star arose in the night. When the Magi departed, he sent more spies to follow them. He was rather pleased with himself that he had deceived them so easily. They had agreed to return at once when they found the new infant king—if indeed there was one to find. Then Herod's thoughts turned again to his age and infirmity.

From an outer point of view, Herod need not have been concerned and depressed; his worldly power was secure. It certainly was well earned—by first-century standards, he had accomplished a great deal. He, Herod, only half Jewish, had gained complete control over his country and had gained for the Jews a real place in the empire. Their religion had been declared a legal one, and they did not have to pay divine homage to the emperor. Herod had established order and law in a land that had been torn by strife for nearly two centuries. Armed brigands were seldom encountered on his excellent roads. The taxes were fair and collected by Jews. Just weights were used in the markets. The Jews as a nation had not had such influence since David's time. Herod encouraged the trades and built a great seaport at Caesarea on the Mediterranean Sea, one of the most important communication centers of the Roman world. He brought the best of Greek culture to his land. The Jewish people could no longer be called barbarians.

In addition, Herod supported the Jewish faith. He had rebuilt the Hebrew Temple in Jerusalem in monumental proportions. The work took forty years to complete, and the new Temple was one of the great buildings of the Roman world. The great stones were so huge and so well fitted together that the foundations of the temple eventually survived twice being razed by the Romans. Two thousand years later, Jews still go and weep beside the foundation walls of that Temple. No leader gave the Jews greater political significance until modern times. It is little wonder that Augustus made Herod a king in spite of his humble lineage. The commoner Herod needed to marry the last princess of the dynasty before him in order to add the aura of legitimacy to the children that followed the marriage, but now he was truly, fully, a king.

Still, Herod had become tired and discouraged. In spite of all he had done for the country, most Jews viewed him as a foreign tyrant. The religious and political leaders paid homage only because it served their best interest. He ruled not through the support and will of his people, but through power, the naked power of a well trained army. He wanted so much to leave a name for himself, to leave a kingly house as his heritage, but he knew he lacked the true loyalty of his people. Then came the Magi on their camels, again shaking his confidence. He was proud to have outwitted them—but then they did not return. His secret police had followed them to Bethlehem and had lost them; one morning they had vanished. The soldiers were given many lashes for their stupidity, and then Herod waited a little longer. He finally realized he had been deceived. Like so many of us, he did not look at the real source of his rage. He rationalized that allowing this child who might be a loving God to live might undermine the hard realities of actual life. He thought to himself (in Auden's words):

Naturally this cannot be allowed to happen. Civilization must be saved even if this means sending for the military, as I suppose it does. How dreary. Why is it that in the end civilization always has to call in these professional tidiers to whom it is all one whether it be Pythagoras or a homicidal lunatic that they are instructed to exterminate. O dear, Why couldn't this wretched infant be born somewhere else? Why can't people be sensible? I don't want to be horrid. Why can't they see that the notion of a finite God is absurd? Because it is. And suppose, just for the sake of argument, that it isn't, that this story is true, that this child is in some inexplicable manner both God and Man, that he grows up, lives, and dies, without committing a single sin? Would that make life any better? On the contrary it would make it far, far worse. For it could only mean this; that once having shown them how, God would expect every man, whatever his fortune, to lead a sinless life in the flesh and on earth. Then indeed would the human race be plunged into madness and despair. And for me personally at this moment it would mean that God had given me the power to destroy Himself. I refuse to be taken in.[1]

Herod quickly concluded the child must die. Since he did not know which child in Bethlehem posed the threat, he would kill them all. He calculated that the child had been born in the past two years. He called in his captain of the guard and calmly issued his order. His directions were brief and to the point: "Go to the village of Bethlehem. A pretender to the royal throne has been born there. Seize every male child two years of age and younger and put them to the sword." An army, in order to be an army, has to be obedient. (Someone has described war as organized insanity.) The soldiers did as they were told. The captain of the troop returned to tell Herod that no child two or under still lived in Bethlehem. Herod was not going to be mocked by any Magi.

For many of us who have never lived in a war-torn land, it is shattering to meditate on this event with a vivid imagination. The event reminds us that in many places in our world today children still die from bombs, racial strife, famine, abandonment; they are also killed by the sword or the gun. As a world society, we still have a long way to go.

The slaughter of the innocents in Bethlehem is one of the most tragic events related in the Bible. Utter despair gripped the little village. The light went out in many lives. The cries of desolation could be heard for miles. Embedded in the story of the Creator's entrance into space and time is this event, which reveals the evil in our world and in us. Matthew sees this tragedy prefigured in Jeremiah's prophecy of Rachel's sorrow for the loss of her children:

> A voice was heard in Ramah,
>   wailing and loud lamentation,
> Rachel weeping for her children;
>   she refused to be consoled,
>   because they are no more.[2]

In Jeremiah's prophecy there was also hope that the children carried away to Babylon would return.

In the slaughter of the innocents, the only possible consolation is a belief in an eternal life in which these children can grow to their full potential. The lonely Christians who faced and suffered martyrdom for three centuries saw these children as the first Christian saints and martyrs. The unmitigated evil of this destruction can be redeemed only by Jesus' resurrection and his picture of the kingdom of heaven. The kingdom of heaven does not explain evil, but it overcomes evil; this horrible event forces us to face the radical evil in our society.

We seldom hear sermons on this event. One student in a seminary class on preaching experienced an existential crisis wrestling with a sermon on this text. Pinchas Lapide, a Jew who lived through the Holocaust, wrote a book supporting the Christian view of the necessity of Jesus' resurrection. Lapide wrote: "All honest theology is a theology of catastrophe, a theology that receives its impulse from the misery and nobility of our human nature."[3] Jesus' resurrection and the reign of heaven are necessary if humans are to make any sense of the slaughter of the innocents as well as Jesus' own crucifixion.

A rational person might ask how a man of Herod's ability and achievements and intellect could be capable of such a disgusting atrocity. Unfortunately, the man who rebuilt the Temple and brought peace to Judea was quite capable of such an act when his power and authority were threatened; indeed, it might have been expected. Herod's violence extended even to his own family. He murdered his wife, whom he adored, and two of his sons, whom he feared were plotting against him. Just five days before his own death, Herod ordered the murder of a third son. The murder of the children in Bethlehem was quite consonant with the historical Herod the Great.

This violent action was possible because Herod was interested in power alone. Human beings whose sole goal is to achieve power and to crush those who oppose them can become as ruthless as Herod. Such ruthlessness may not always literally result in murder. However, all the great conquerors, from Attila the Hun through Genghis Khan to Stalin and Hitler, have shed blood as if it were water. In an early story of the beginning of our universe, the source of evil—one of the brightest and best of the angelic beings—decided that this power could run heaven better than God; Lucifer rose in revolt. This attitude has contaminated our human society. When we think we can run our lives better than the Holy One can, we are likely to fall into bad company. This truth applies in our homes, social life, business, politics, as well as in war.

However, Herod's bloody rage was ineffective. In the end, the Eternal One is not mocked; divine power is stronger than any human or evil power. A messenger of the Holy One of Israel warned Joseph in a dream that Herod was searching for the baby Jesus to destroy him. Joseph listened. The instructions seemed absurd, but the message was filled with numinous power; Joseph knew how to listen to more than his own petty reason. He got up from his dream and made ready to flee. Mary never questioned. As the family sped out into the night, the cold wind of winter desert pierced the baby's garments and Jesus cried. Had Joseph not listened to his inspiration, Jesus would have never grown up. Jesus would not have been able to give us the wisdom that he alone could give. He would not have confronted the powers of evil on Golgotha and defeated them. Christmas needs Easter, but Easter also needs the mystery of the Creator entering our world as a baby at Christmas.

Herod and his soldiers, bent on destruction in Bethlehem, confront us with the awful mystery of evil in our world and in human society. Herod is a tragic symbol of human egotism that will have its way at all costs. Herod was so fearful that something would stand between him and his personal will that he struck out at anyone who might question his authority, even babies. Herod's soldiers were so obedient to their ruler that they shared in his evil. They also feared for their lives if they did not obey their king's command. They were in the same position as the Roman soldiers that nailed Jesus to the cross. They remind us how careful we need to be in giving our final allegiance to any person, idea, or cause.

When we truly face the significance of the slaughter of the children in Bethlehem (the ugly, dark stain in Herod's world and in our world), we are forced to make one of several choices. We can simply say the world and the society in which we live are meaningless and we should expect tragedy and mayhem; then we are justified in grabbing what we can in any way we can as we wait for extinction. Another choice is to deny the reality of evil; according to this view, tragedy is just a fantasy our minds have created. Evil then is just in the minds of those who believe it is real; as we become more mature, we see only love and good. A third choice is to act like Job's comforters and tell people that any evil that befalls them is just payment for their sins in this life or in a previous one. According to this view, people in trouble need to acknowledge their sins and get right with the Deity; through suffering they are punished, corrected, and given growth. All these attitudes make mockery of the enormous human pain and agony in our broken world.

If we follow any of these three choices, we are likely to deny the reality of human evil in ourselves, to blind ourselves to the Herod, Pilate, or Hitler within us. If we refuse to see the dark stain within us, we give it power to act without our control, to act autonomously through us. Then the darkness within us can strike at us in depression or anxiety, or we can project our evil side onto other people and see them as the problem. Freud answered Einstein's question, "Why is there war?" with words like these: "War is inevitable; if human beings did not strike at other people in war, their inner death wish would turn against them and human beings would commit suicide."[4]

Fortunately, there is a fourth choice. We can face the Herod within us, excruciatingly painful as that process is. Those who are fighting evil in the world need to be particularly aware of their own evil. Alison Curry, a tutor in the South African Idasa's Training Centre for Democracy, has written:

> As activists many of us were so busy waging a larger war—against that amorphous enemy "the system"—that we did not have the time, energy or inclination to look within. The enemy was too large. To indulge in criticizing our leaders or, even less, ourselves, was seen as contradictory to the whole impetus of involvement . . . We can only begin to meet the challenges of the 1990's when we start to develop a new culture—a culture of looking within which involves a very different risk to facing the tear gas of the past.[5]

Most saints have considered themselves the worst of sinners, because the more they knew of the Divine, the more they realized their imperfections that kept them from full discipleship.

We can control the imperfection and evil we find in the world only when we realize these things are deep within us too. Then we can seek the power of the risen Jesus, who defeated evil and death and is available to us when we turn toward him in quiet and prayer. Then we will contribute less and less to the misery of the world. We will be able to reach out to the homeless, the psychologically broken, the starving, those in prisons, and those in bombed cities. We also will recognize and accept that we cannot meet all the world's need.

How can we avoid being overwhelmed when we look at the innumerable problems of the world? How do we decide what is our calling in caring for others? We can begin with Mother Teresa's answer to the question: "How can you continue your work when you realize that you are reaching only one percent of the dying in Calcutta?" She replied: "I was not called to be successful; I was only called to be faithful."[6]

We need time for reflection and quiet as we look at our lives in the fellowship of the risen Jesus. We also need a fellowship of Christian peers with whom we can share our lives, people who will be caring enough to call our blind spots to our attention. The Church of the Saviour in Washington, D.C., has made a real impact on the slums in which it is located, providing teaching, affordable and decent housing, a retreat center, a potter's house (a restaurant-bookstore where the hungry can eat), a ministry of taking people to visit the poorer places in the world, and hospitals for indigent men released from hospitals and unable to care for themselves. One hundred and forty members of this church have been able to accomplish such work because each member is required to belong to a mission group in which people pray together, listen to each other, plan together, and work together. Gordon Cosby, who founded the Church of the Saviour, drew his inspiration from John Wesley's little manual on religious group fellowship. Wesley's class meetings transformed the very life of Great Britain at the end of the eighteenth century and produced a society able to defeat Napoleon.[7]

We need to know the incredible love of the risen Christ in prayer and sacrament. We need to realize that we can bring all of ourselves into the presence of the Holy One; we need fellowship to give us support and guidance in our spiritual growth. We also must reach out to misery caused by the Herods of our time. We must take seriously Baron von Hugel's suggestion that service to the poor is an essential part of our spiritual life. Von Hugel insisted to Evelyn Underhill that in addition to her intense prayer life, she was to spend some time each week working in the soup kitchens in the slums of London. Dealing with the Herod within is part of our lifetime spiritual journey.[8]

10

Cosmic Tentacles of Brilliance

The Holy One entered into creation as a baby in a stable in Bethlehem. A new age dawned; love became incarnate as a human being. Amazing as this event was, however, it was not God's only self-revelation: For fifteen billion years the Holy One had been preparing for this moment, and the Creator began sending cosmic tentacles of brilliance out to human beings as soon as they were conscious enough to hear and feel the touch of the Holy One.

Abraham heard the call of divine love and set out like the Magi on a perilous journey. Jacob, fleeing from his brother's wrath, built an altar at the place where the heavens opened, and he saw the ladder to heaven with angels descending and ascending on it. The patriarch Joseph listened to his dreams and listened even more carefully as the cosmic tentacles of brilliance interpreted these visions of the night for him. Through these divine messages Joseph, sold as a slave in Egypt, saved his family, which grew into a great nation. Moses met the Holy One of Israel in the bush that burned and was not consumed. This reluctant prophet led his people out of Egypt to their own land and warned them to listen to their dreams, the dark speech of the spirit in which the Holy One often spoke.

Greek and Hebrew people, far more than most Western people until very recent times, deeply believed the world of spirit penetrates the physical one. Most modern European languages have few words to describe human fellowship with the world of the Spirit and the Divine. In the Hebrew language, the dream of God, the vision of the Holy One, the message from an encounter with an angel, and the call of God can hardly be distinguished from one another. In the Greek New Testament twelve different words describe human fellowship and communication with the realm of the Spirit. In one passage of the New Testament, an appearance of an angel is described as a vision; in a related passage, the same experience is described as a dream; in a third description, the text speaks of an encounter with God. These rich descriptions suggest that human beings have ecstasies in which they touch a realm of reality different from that provided by the five physical senses, such as Peter had on the rooftop in Joppa. The New Testament speaks of revelations in which a nonphysical realm of reality is revealed or unveiled, uncovered.[1]

Most of the important characters of the Christmas story were led, guided, and saved by their dreams or by angelic messages. We can scarcely make sense of the story if we reject or ignore such experiences. Only in the account of the resurrection of Jesus do we find a similar emphasis on angelic appearances.

What we sing often reveals more of the depth of the soul than what we think we believe. On Christmas Eve something bubbles up out of us as we sing the ancient carols. These songs echo what the angel chorus sang to the startled shepherds—a song that human ears had longed to hear from the beginning of time: "Gloria in excelsis Deo."

> Glory to God in the highest heaven,
> and to earth peace among those God favors.[2]

Few Christian hymns touch us more than our Christmas carols; they are effervescent with divine love and with the angelic experiences that made possible the Christmas narrative. These carols bypass our minds and touch our souls; Christmas would be barren without these tentacles of brilliance that shine through the birth of Jesus like a thread of gold. Few of us have hearts so hardened that a chord is not struck within the deepest part of the human soul when we really hear the angelic message. At the risk of being repetitious, let us listen to many songs we sing at Christmas with such joy and notice how many speak of the angels' choirs. Pause and listen to these songs as we heap one song on another until we see a blazing bonfire of praise and joy.[3]

> Angels we have heard on high,
>   Singing sweetly through the night,
> And the mountains in reply
>   Echoing their brave delight.
> Gloria in excelsis Deo. (42,1)

Another ancient carol concludes its message in Latin:

> And thus that manger poor
>   Became a throne;
> For he whom Mary bore
>   Was God the Son.
> O come, then, let us join
>   The heavenly host,

To praise the Father, Son,
　　And Holy Ghost.
Venite adoramus Dominum. (41,4)

The first Nowell the angel did say
　　Was to certain poor shepherds in fields as they lay;
In fields as they lay, keeping their sheep,
　　On a cold winter's night that was so deep.
　　　Nowell, Nowell, Nowell, Nowell,
　　　Born is the King of Israel. (30,1)

All my heart this night rejoices
　　As I hear, far and near,
Sweetest angel voices.
"Christ is born," their choirs are singing,
　　Till the air everywhere
Now with joy is ringing. (32,1)

　　The angelic choirs—tentacles of brilliance—sing for sheer joy, welcoming the new divine light:

What child is this, who laid to rest,
　　On Mary's lap is sleeping?
Whom angels greet with anthems sweet,
　　While shepherds watch are keeping?
　　This, this is Christ the King,
　　　Whom shepherds guard and angels sing:
　　Haste, haste to bring him laud,
　　　The babe, the son of Mary. (36,1)

Hark! the herald angels sing
Glory to the newborn King!
Peace on earth and mercy mild,
God and sinners reconciled!
Joyful, all ye nations, rise,
Join the triumph of the skies;
With the angelic host proclaim
Christ is born in Bethlehem!
　　Hark! the herald angels sing
　　Glory to the newborn King! (27,1)

And still the angel hosts sing on:

Angels, from the realms of glory,
　　Wing your flights o'er all the earth;
Ye, who sang creation's story,
　　Now proclaim Messiah's birth:
　　Come and worship, Come and worship,
　　Worship Christ, the newborn King. (28,1)

For Christ is born of Mary,
  And gathered all above,
While mortals sleep, the angels keep
  Their watch of wondering love.
O morning stars, together
  Proclaim the holy birth!
And praises sing to God the King,
  And peace to all on earth. (21,2)

When heaven touches earth, it reaches into the deepest crannies of the human soul. Heaven came down to earth in angelic choirs and messages and also in the Creator's coming down among us and being born like one of us. Three more carols express the joy that only poetry can express.

It came upon the midnight clear,
  That glorious song of old,
From angels bending near the earth
  To touch their harps of gold:
"Peace on the earth, good will to all
  From heaven's all-gracious King"
The world in solemn stillness lay
  To hear the angels sing. (19,1)

While shepherds watched their flocks by night,
  All seated on the ground,
The angel of the Lord came down,
  And glory shone around.

"Fear not," said he, for mighty dread
  Had seized their troubled mind;
"Glad tidings of great joy I bring
  To you and humankind." (13,1,2)

  Sing, choirs of angels,
  Sing in exultation,
Sing, all ye citizens of heav'n above;
  Glory to God
  In the highest;
  O come, let us adore him,
  O come, let us adore him.
  O come, let us adore him, Christ the Lord. (12,3)

The Spiritual and Angelic Realm

These poetic words—particularly when set to emotionally charged music—can touch us profoundly and trigger emotions we did not know we had. We human beings are in touch with many different levels of reality. We have been brought up in a one-dimensional world, taught that only matter is real and that unconditional love is a rarity if not an impossibility. Most of us in our time have been starved for experiences of the divine love that these hymns proclaim. The deepest recesses of our souls, however, know that we can be in touch with such a spiritual dimension. Singing carols about the angels of Christmas brings us back in touch with the world of Spirit as that realm was concretely incarnated in our world in that Bethlehem stable. But do these Christmas angels about which we sing have any real meaning for us, or are they meaningless, sentimental images? I very much fear that if these angels are a pious fiction, an imaginative fancy, then the birth of Christ in Bethlehem is itself but a quaint old legend—and the birth of Christ in our hearts is also merely an imaginative fantasy, an emotional wish that cannot really take place.

I, for one, believe in the reality of these experiences—in the messages of divine love and in the divine messengers through whom the Holy One reaches out to us from the infinite world of Spirit. This spiritual dimension penetrates our lives and every part of our physical world. The birth of the Creator as a baby in Bethlehem is the most concrete example of the divine presence in our universe, and I am convinced that this same Christ wants to be born in me and in every human heart today.

Yet a strange truth is that those who are not aware of the demonic in themselves, the Herod within, also are seldom aware of the angelic dimension penetrating our world or of the divine child who longs to be born in each of us—and even in our enemies. So many of us cut ourselves off from conscious awareness of this whole realm of reality that extends beyond our physical existence and our ego-consciousness. Sadly, such unconsciousness leaves us cut off from the angelic and prey to the demonic. But the creative Spirit cannot be forced on us; love and freedom are always joined together, and the Creator lovingly gives us the freedom and power to shut ourselves off from the spiritual realm and even from the love of the Holy One.

Victor White, a distinguished Dominican scholar and a friend of psychiatrist C. G. Jung, points out that it is impossible to delete the demonic and angelic from the New Testament:

"The polite efforts of the nineteenth-century Liberal criticism to exorcise the demons [and angels] of the New Testament, to explain away its more "devilish" passages as a later and superstitious adulteration of the pure ethical milk of the gospel, or at least to apologize for them as an unimportant concession to contemporary illusions, have proved a dismal failure.[4]

White goes on to write that even the most radical biblical critics "hold that these passages belong to the most primitive strata, the essential core of the evangelical tradition." So if we take the New Testament seriously, we must deal with its spiritual dimension.

Thomas Aquinas, the greatest of medieval thinkers and one of the greatest thinkers of all times, has been called the angelic doctor—not because of his holy life, but rather because of his profound teaching about angels. Those of our century who think Thomas was naive about angels simply betray that they have never bothered to read him. Few of these enlightened ones could claim even in their wildest moments to greater breadth of mind than Thomas, yet they poke fun at ideas in a superior way and laugh at theological debates about how many angels can dance on the head of a pin, an idea that would have been ludicrous to Thomas as well.

Only the most uninformed think angels are material, concrete beings. They are spiritual realities that reveal themselves to women and men in moments of vision, and that also break in on human consciousness in dreams, flooding it with awareness and wonder and fear.

Angels are, according to Thomas, *intelligibilia intelligentia*. They are thinking thoughts imbued with power. They are nonmaterial reality, spiritual reality, though they can interact with and influence physical reality. This interpretation of nonphysical and physical is mirrored by the human mind, which has powers of knowing beyond the five physical senses but which also has power to direct substantial, material bodies.

Carl Jung, who opened his mind to so many things, discovered in his psychiatric practice that there are strange nonphysical realities that torment and also transform the human mind. He called these realities "complexes" and "archetypes"; Aquinas and the early church called them "angels" and "demons."

The important thing is not the terminology but the realization that there are such powers, powers of numinous strength and majesty, that can break in on humans. These powers stir the deepest and most awesome responses within us; they can destroy or upbuild, illumine or darken. Those who do not recognize them, who persistently refuse to admit their existence, have little chance to avoid the destructive powers in the human psyche and in the universe; they are unlikely to open themselves to the angelic, and to the Christ who wants to live within all humans.

There are dimensions of life far deeper and more mysterious than most of us usually admit. Those who have the courage to open themselves to these Christmas angels may come to know divine love more deeply. They may be able to reach deep into life and know its meaning more fully.

The Christmas angels are not absurd, for the Spirit that fills holy seasons like Easter and Christmas helps us realize that life and living are not as simple as we sometimes think. We realize we are surrounded by mysteries and marvels so great that they can make even us change our lives. We may recognize that we need to love one another as the Holy One loves us; this can force us to a new way of life.

When we remember and relive the events of Bethlehem, the powers of heaven come close. The veil that separates us from the world of the Spirit is drawn back. Whenever God breaks through, we are surrounded by angelic powers.

On a cold night some two thousand years ago, the Creator emerged into creation and took human flesh to reveal to us the way to human fulfillment—the path of prayer and love. All the angels sang, all the powers of heaven flooded forth in joy. May we taste something of that joy throughout the year.

The Holy One Continues
to Reach Out to Us

Angelic events surrounded Jesus' resurrection as well.[5] Angels met and frightened the women as they came to prepare Jesus' dead body for burial, though Mary Magdalene was so overcome with grief when she met two angels at the tomb that she did not realize their heavenly quality and so was not even frightened. Jesus' resurrected body itself had angelic characteristics. Although he ate the fish and bread that he was offered, he also moved through stout locked doors. And the angelic experiences continued in the early church. Jesus appeared in an angelic, numinous way to Paul on the road to Damascus. An angel also appeared to Cornelius; that experience changed Peter's life and the life of the entire early church. Most early church leaders were led by their dreams and their visions of angels, and this practice continued through the most vital and traumatic period of the church's life. One early church leader shows his great respect for dreams when he writes that God only speaks in visions to those who are too stubborn to listen to their dreams. Reverence for the dream as a communication from the Divine never ceased in the Eastern Orthodox Church and is very much alive there today; the idea that the Holy One no longer speaks to ordinary people through angels, dreams, and visions gradually emerged only as the thinking of scholasticism took over the Western world.[6]

After three hundred years of intermittent persecution, the Emperor Constantine abolished the malicious brutality under which Christians had lived. In the year 312, Constantine saw a flaming symbol in the sky and heard the words, "In this sign you will conquer." He did not understand the symbol. A few days later, Christ appeared to the emperor in a dream, carrying a cross like the symbol ☧; he revealed to Constantine that the symbol was made from the first two letters of the word "Christ" in Greek (the X [chi] stands for "Ch" and the P [rho] stands for "r"). Constantine won the battle against the pagan contender for the empire, and from then on this strange cross became the symbol of the later Roman Empire. (The church theologian, Lactantius, recorded this event within a year of its occurrence.) Do such visions still occur?

The German Lutheran Church gathered in solemn conclave shortly after World War II. One of the first subjects on the agenda was the question: "Had the church contributed in any way to the rise of the Nazi movement in Germany?" After a day's debate, the assembly concluded the church was blameless. But the church was forced to reassess this conclusion when Martin Niemoller, a Lutheran minister who had been imprisoned for opposing Hitler and was a hero of the church and of the German people, had a profound, numinous experience. The night the assembly reached its conclusion, Niemoller was awakened and saw before him a light, which was unmistakably the light of the holy, the Divine One. Niemoller was tremendously moved, and then he heard behind him the unmistakable voice of Adolf Hitler saying: "Martin, Martin, why didn't you ever tell me?" As Niemoller became fully awake, he reflected on the many times he had been eyeball to eyeball with Hitler, and never once had he tried to lay the claim of Christ on him. Martin Niemoller told his dream to the assembled church, and two days later the Synod passed a resolution stating that the church was as responsible for the rise of the Nazi party as any other part of German society. Niemoller had pushed the group truly to face its shadow side.[7]

One of the most influential modern theologians, Henri Nouwen, has taught in some of the best theological schools in the United States. He left the academic world, however, to work with disadvantaged people. On a snowy day in 1988, he was struck down by a truck and nearly died. He had a near-death experience, and he found himself in the presence of Jesus, who was extremely personal and yet was at the same time embracing the universe. I have read few more moving and well-articulated visions of the kingdom of heaven than Nouwen's description of his experience. Nouwen says that until he had this vision of Christ, his theology had started with experiences of human love and then moved toward divine love. His profound encounter with the Divine showed him that his task in theology was to start with this experience of unconditional love and life; somehow he must find words to share this message with other human beings.[8]

At about the same time that Nouwen received this vision, a friend of mine in Texas also had a near brush with death and wrote me of her experience of the angelic realm. She described the same experience of unconditional love about which Nouwen wrote so eloquently.

Wherever I lecture and let people know that I believe in the angelic realm, men and women come forward to tell me of their encounters with the angelic. At a conference in May 1993, a woman wrote that she had seen an angelic figure when she was a lonely three-year-old; this was one of the most encouraging and sustaining experiences of her entire life. One of the most impressive descriptions of such an experience I have encountered was written out for me by a woman with a rare gift for poetic prose.

> It was a pretty pre-dawn morning filled with the fragrance of spring when I was suddenly to find myself wide awake and sitting bolt upright in my bed. The room had taken on a rare atmosphere glistening with a white light tinged with gold. An air of expectancy permeated the room, so much that it made me turn my gaze questioningly to the window at my left, then to those directly across from me, and at that moment, just to the right, this scene appeared.
>
> Two beings of stately yet gentle bearing, almost as tall as the room is high in that area, stood facing each other on either side of a large doorway. They were clothed, each one, in a soft, flowing, opaque garment with a radiance resembling sunshine on snow tinged with a faint pink. Their arms seemed wing-like, reaching from their shoulders almost to the floor.
>
> They stood silent and motionless, and yet in a state of expectancy (I seemed to sense) until a feminine figure garbed in a darker hue came into view, with head bent slightly down and forward as if slowly ascending from a lower level. They then moved to enfold her, almost caressingly—and I distinctly saw the smiling face of our mother and heard her familiar voice laughingly say, as if a bit breathlessly, "I've finally made it!" She seemed happy. The smile remained on her face as, still enfolded in their embrace, she and the two beings *glided* by me . . . just inches from the foot of my bed. I reached out to touch her. My heart cried, "Mother! Mother, don't you see me?" Taking no notice of me, they glided on by and out of sight.
>
> The room was still scintillating. In fact my whole being seemed charged with a force I had not before known. I fell back on my pillow in wonderment. What did it all mean? After a time—how long I don't remember—my reasoning mind found an answer. "She really *is* better—she really *is* going to be well." I was rejoicing. I felt electrified—even the room seemed electrified. I don't know any other word to describe it. I wanted to tell my husband. I *must* tell him the good news. But, no—it was too early to awaken him. He needed his rest, and it would keep.
>
> The atmosphere in the room was changing now, becoming more normal, although it still seemed all aglow. As a matter of fact, this lasted to a degree for several days. Presently the ringing of the telephone awakened my husband, and from his response I sensed the message conveyed by his brother-in-law: "Your mother has just passed away."
>
> Mr. Kelsey, I do not feel I have done justice to the experience. Words are so inadequate. It is an experience I do not forget. It did something fine to my consciousness. I wish I might paint a picture of those Angelic Beings! Even now, the mere thought of them stirs my soul. . . . [9]

Since men and women are touched by such transforming experiences today, there is little reason to doubt the reality of the angelic experiences recorded in New Testament narratives about Jesus' death and resurrection. Our Christmas hymns describe a world more fully real than the materialistic world in which so many of us have been brainwashed. The drama of Christmas may well be giving us one of our deepest glimpses into the heart of the Creator.

11

Augustus Caesar
and Jesus Crucified

The essential message of Christmas is strange and radical. It proclaims a truth that few human beings take seriously. In Bethlehem, the Creator slipping into creation announces: "The world and its magnificence are not ultimately important or significant; the really significant humans are those who live by the Spirit of the Holy One expressed in the life and teaching of Jesus of Nazareth." History bears out this strange proclamation that worldly magnificence in the end means very little. Mary, the mother of Jesus, was speaking a profound truth when she prophesied:

> The Holy One has scattered the proud in the imagination of
> their hearts.
> The Holy one has put down the mighty from their thrones
> and exalted those of low degree.[1]

In the second chapter of his gospel Luke begins his account of the birth of Jesus with a delightful and subtle irony: "In those days a decree went out from Emperor Augustus that all the world should be registered. This was the first registration and was taken while Quirinius was governor of Syria."[2] Luke's mention of the great Augustus and his representative in Syria is merely a setting in which the jewel is displayed. He mentions these two rulers for two reasons: He wants the reader to know he is writing history and not fantasy, and he also wants to provide the proper backdrop for the staging of his drama. Luke makes no further mention of either of these two men. Although they were important in their day, by the time Luke wrote his gospel (some seventy or eighty years after Jesus' birth), Quirinius was such a hazy figure and so insignificant that Luke placed this once powerful man in the wrong time and province. While Quirinius was living, people trembled in their sandals at the mention of his name; when he was in power, his word was law and whole nations were in terror of him. But in less than a century he was so completely forgotten that a careful scholar like Luke could not be exactly sure who he was.

History has a tendency to turn the importance of people upside down. As we have already indicated, Augustus was the most powerful emperor the Western world had known up to his time. All the known world, except Persia, was under his control. Had Hitler or Napoleon consolidated his power into an empire that lasted for a thousand years, then he might have been comparable to Augustus. Augustus took over Rome as a city of brick and left it a metropolis of marble; his engineers built roads that linked all parts of the empire and that are still a marvel of efficiency.

The Roman legions kept peace within the empire and repelled any attempts of barbarians to enter it. Milestones and pillars were erected along these roads providing travelers precise directions. Augustus's navy policed the Mediterranean and Black Seas; people could travel safely from Spain to the Caspian Sea, from North Africa to the Rhine River. Piracy disappeared. Mail moved from one part of the empire to another. In addition, Augustus built new cities and rebuilt ancient ones at strategic points in the interior of his empire. These cities dominated the new roads and became centers of Roman power. The coinage bearing Augustus's image was standard through the empire. (I have worn a tie tack made from a denarius bearing his image for years, and no one has as yet identified the head of Augustus Caesar that once was known by everyone.)

In his time and for hundreds of years, Augustus was the epitome of world power and magnificence, power and law. In addition, even while he lived this man was worshiped as a god. People in all parts of the empire burned incense before his statue as before a divinity. Poets fought for the opportunity to sing his praise. Some of the greatest Latin poetry was devoted to honoring this great man. All the arts flourished. People living then thought life had reached its apogee. Augustus was one whose memory or name would never fade.

In the tiny kingdom of Judea, favored by Augustus because of Herod's political help, a peasant woman gave birth to a child rumored to be illegitimate. The woman and the man who accompanied her had so little influence that they were forced to seek refuge in a stable when the woman gave birth. Silly gossip in Herod's court led the paranoid king to try to destroy the child. Like harried animals the family fled by night to Egypt to save the infant's life. In Egypt they lived as refugees until Herod died; then the family returned to Nazareth in Galilee (most Jews viewed Galileans as second-class citizens). Jesus learned the carpenter's trade and went to synagogue school. At twenty-nine he left home to follow the call that spoke from the depth of him. Jesus left his bench and tools, bid farewell to his family, and went off to be baptized in the Jordan by John the Baptist.

From there he went into the wild and barren desert above the Dead Sea to discern his mission, after first tussling with tempting demonic voices. His call was clear; he gathered together a band of followers, common folk for the most part—though at least one, John, was a profoundly mystical and highly educated man, probably one of the religious leaders of Israel.[3]

Jesus' ministry was an instant success; he preached to large crowds, healed multitudes of sick people, and proclaimed that the kingdom of heaven was at hand. He trained his followers in his ministry of teaching, preaching, and healing. These men and women were amazed at the power that flowed through them as they followed their master. Jesus traveled through Judea and Galilee and even went as far north as Tyre and Sidon. His ministry lasted less than three years. He never owned a home, and he said to someone who wanted to follow him: "Foxes have holes, and birds of the air have nests; but the Son of Man has nowhere to lay his head."[4] At the Passover, A.D. 33, Jesus of Nazareth set his face toward Jerusalem and his disciples shrank back in fear; he had told them what lay in wait for them. After a triumphant entry into the holy city, Jesus cleansed the Temple of those who bought and sold there. This action convinced the leaders of the Temple that Jesus must be destroyed. They bribed one of his disciples to betray him with a kiss. Jesus, anticipating his death, had one final fellowship meal with his disciples; then he was seized by the Temple guard in the Garden of Gethsemane and taken before the religious authorities of his own people. He was condemned to death and turned over to Pilate, the Roman governor, who alone could carry out the death sentence. Pilate had Jesus crucified between two thieves. Jesus died and was buried in the tomb of Joseph of Arimathea. His followers claimed that he had risen from death and had appeared to them as a transcendently vital, living human person.

From the view of the historians of that time or from a strictly materialistic point of view, it would be mad to compare the stature and significance of these two, Augustus and Jesus of Nazareth. From either point of view there could be no ground for even bringing the man of Nazareth into the august presence of the mighty emperor—even as an academic exercise. As a matter of fact, only one of the Roman historians of that time even mentions Jesus. Yet the truth is this, the bald historical truth: the only reason most people today have ever heard of Augustus Caesar is that he was part of the historical background for the birth of Jesus of Nazareth.

Jesus has kept the memory of Augustus alive as a shadowy figure who flits furtively across the stage of the divine drama of Christmas. Had Jesus not been born in Augustus's reign, the great emperor would be remembered only by a few scholars of ancient Western history. Indeed, the eminent historian Arnold Toynbee pointed out that the entire history of Europe is linked to the Christian story more than to Roman culture; Europe *is* Christianity. Christianity came to life and finally became the established religion of the Roman Empire; nearly everything European has been touched and changed by the stable-born child from Nazareth. For those of us with a European heritage, Jesus is at the very root of our culture.

Augustus laid the foundations of a peaceful empire in which the vital Christian communities could develop. However, because the Christians were not a legal religion and would not acknowledge the Roman emperors as God, they were persecuted, tortured, or thrown into the Colosseum to be torn apart by hungry wild beasts. (The government viewed as treason any refusal to pay homage to the emperor as God.) Christianity survived because it gave meaning to a society that had lost its sense of purpose. Life without meaning or destiny did not satisfy the rulers, the rich, or the educated—or the poor or the slaves who made up more than half of the population of the empire. Christianity grew and flourished.

During the time of persecution, those Christian families who were betrayed by informers as being Christians faced a terrible fate: The husband was put to death (often in the arena); the wife and children were sold into slavery; the family property was sold, and all the proceeds from these transactions were given to the informer. In spite of this intermittent persecution for three-hundred years, the fellowship of Christians grew. Spectators at the arena were amazed at the fearlessness with which the Christians died; the blood of the martyrs was indeed the seed of the church. Many also were struck by the way these people loved one another. Their faith gave these Christians a new kind of caring and hope and joy in the face even of death. The new Way grew because it gave hope to those who felt hopeless—slaves, common people, and even some of the best minds in the empire. Slowly Christian communities grew until they took over the Roman Empire. This power emanated from a birth in a stable and the victory of Jesus' resurrection, two parts of one story.[5]

For several centuries, most educated people would have mocked the idea that Jesus and his followers could be compared to the mighty monarch, Augustus. Caesar's power and significance lay in his well-trained army, in the many kingdoms that he ruled, in the roads that he built, in his magnificent marble cities and the milestones that guided people to them. But Augustus's palaces have long since fallen. Some of his most important roads are buried under yards of shifting dust and sand. His milestones are cryptic curiosities unearthed by archaeologists in unexpected places. Most of Augustus's great cities are mounds of dirt. Many of them are as totally forgotten as the ancient city of Paestum. It was discovered only by chance after World War II when Italian contractors came upon a great amphitheater and then a whole city when they were excavating for a new road.

The stable-born refugee, itinerant preacher who ended his ordinary human life on a criminal's cross has made a far greater impact on history than the mighty and glorious Augustus. Some of the world's most magnificent temples have been raised by Jesus' followers. Some of the world's greatest sculpture, painting, and poetry have been created to tell his story. Agrippa and Augustus built the innovative and spectacular Pantheon to honor their gods; ironically, this building still stands and has been a Christian church for sixteen hundred years. For over two thousand years the numbers of Jesus' followers have continued to increase. Recently, in Singapore, Korea, and China, Jesus has attracted followers with some of the same enthusiasm as was shown by the early Christians. More and more men and women are testifying to the vital power of the Spirit that the risen Jesus has poured out on his followers.

Jesus has left his mark on humankind because he embodied the spiritual power of the Creator, a power that fully entered the human scene through Jesus' birth in Bethlehem. Jesus showed the human world how the Holy One would act as a human being. Jesus' words and actions continued those of Mary and Joseph, and extended them: a life of mercy, love, devotion, courage, healing, and resurrection. The Roman world tried to crush the early church, but it was indestructible; neither the naked power of the sadistic world nor the gates of hell could prevail against it. Augustus and Jesus: the world and the Spirit. It is very difficult for those of us conditioned by a materialistic culture to believe truly the message of Christmas: The Creator of the universe loves our world and its people and became a human being to reveal the ultimate meaning of reality to us. Thank God for the great panorama of history on which the Creator has painted this truth; if we look carefully at the limitless expanse of the canvas of time, we can see the Creator's bold strokes portraying the meaning of creation.

If we know our history and reflect on it, we have little reason to be surprised that spiritual power is ultimately far more enduring than political, financial, or material power. Few of us can name the dynasty of the powerful emperor of China at the time of Confucius; yet Confucius's spiritual writings have shaped Chinese lives for twenty-five hundred years. Only Chinese scholars can tell us the emperor of that great land when Jesus was born, and yet Jesus' teachings have a growing impact on China. Lao-tzu gave China the religion of Taoism, but even scholars know nothing of the political history of his times. The princes of India who smiled indulgently on Buddha when he set out to reform the ancient Hindu religion are forgotten. The religious conquests of Muhammad and his followers reshaped the map of the world, and now half a billion Muslims hear Muhammad's Koran recited daily; but few people know the sultans who created the Arabic Empire. Almost no one can name the kings of Europe when Francis of Assisi began to preach and practice the love of God—even the incredibly powerful pope at the time of Brother Francis is forgotten—and still millions of modern men and women pray the simple prayer attributed to Francis. Who ruled Denmark when Kierkegaard wrote from his heart? Who were the princes who protected Luther from what pope? What were the political conditions when Augustine wrote *The City of God*? The stories and words of the great religious leaders of Israel—Moses, Amos, Isaiah, and Jeremiah—are read by millions today, while the mighty kings who ruled them are remembered only because these religious leaders lived in their time.

In one baptismal service, adult candidates for baptism were asked if they would "renounce the devil and all his works, the vain pomp and glory of the world, with all covetous desires of the same, and the sinful desires of the flesh."[6] In asking this question, the church was not being restrictive; rather, it was pointing out that the lives of those who have these goals as their primary objectives have minimal abiding significance. The lives of those who focus on the "pomp and glory of the world"—like Augustus Caesar—have become only shadows. Jesus of Nazareth was not restrictive, but realistic. In his teaching and in his life Jesus pointed out that those who live only in "this world" reap dust and ashes. Those who try to follow Jesus and live in the Spirit reap a reality greater than human imagination can describe.

Whenever we pray Jesus' prayer, the Lord's Prayer, we conclude with these words: "For the kingdom, and the power, and the glory are yours now and forever." In these words we are praying and affirming that might and majesty and holiness belong to the Creator who entered this world to show us the true nature of eternal life, to reveal the things that have true abiding meaning. But do we mean these words when we say them? What we do better indicates what we believe than what we say, and too many of us focus most of our attention on the worldly and ephemeral. Jesus calls us to remember that the true significance of our lives lies not in our worldly fame or appearance or in the splash we make in the social whirl, or even in our correct statements of dogma, but in how much our actions reflect the love expressed in Jesus Christ. At the first Christmas, God slipped into our world in a humble stable to give us a new way to value the importance of what we do and are.

One problem with the yearly celebrations of our Christian festivals is that we tend to forget Christmas is *always* with us, with its strange message that God is love and that the Holy One is always trying to draw us into the orbit of divine love. The message of Easter is much the same: The Creator came into the world and defeated the powers of evil—of death and discord—and opened the kingdom of heaven to all of us who will receive it. We can go the old way of building larger and larger barns and gaining more and more power, until this world has passed and we find ourselves plaintive phantoms weeping among the ruins. Or we can celebrate Christmas and Easter all year and take seriously the call to humility and love, to courage and prayer, leaving our lasting mark on this world and at the same time moving toward the ineffable infinity of eternal life. Augustus Caesar or Jesus of Nazareth? The final act of the Christmas drama is the resurrection of Jesus. This historical event completes the meaning of the birth in the stable and helps us make a decision.

12

The Grand Finale

In any great drama, we are held in tension until the last scene of the last act and the curtain has fallen on the stage. Until then, we cannot be sure whether we are watching a comedy or a tragedy. In Goethe's *Faust* the viewer cannot imagine how Faust could be saved until the final scene. (We noted in chapter 8 that Faust was rescued from the clutches of Mephistopheles by three redeemed spirits sent by the Virgin Mary.) Without this climactic scene the play would have been the ghastly tragedy it was in Christopher Marlowe's earlier version (*Doctor Faustus*), rather than one of the greatest human expressions of heaven's redemptive power. The real distinction between a comedy and a tragedy is clear: In tragedy the forces of evil, violence, destruction, and hatred are victors; in comedy the action of the play passes through defeat to victory, and the tension of the plot is resolved by forgiveness, reconciliation, and redemption.

This distinction is illustrated in Shakespeare's last and most hopeful dramas, *The Winter's Tale*, *Cymbeline*, and *The Tempest*. In each of these plays, a potentially confused and tragic situation is transformed and redeemed in the last act by kindness, forgiveness, and mercy; the plays conclude in a tide of hope and peace. Similarly, Dante's unparalleled dramatic poem begins in the dark wood, plunges the author and reader through the depths of hell and then leads them up through purgatory, and ends with an ascent into the highest heaven. His poem is usually called *The Divine Comedy*; Dante simply called it *The Comedy*.

The birth of the Creator as a baby into our broken world would have been one of the bleakest of all tragedies if Jesus' life had ended on the cross and in the tomb. Cosmic creative love would have been defeated; evil and darkness would have conquered. If that had been the end of the Creator's cosmic drama, Paul's judgment about Christians who do not believe in Jesus' resurrection would have been true: They "are of all people most to be pitied."[1] But the cosmic drama did not and does not end on the cross and in the tomb. The Creator had prepared an unbelievably magnificent, majestic, hopeful, and reassuring last act for those who will see the drama through to the end. I do not like to heap adjectives one upon another, but the final scenes of the Creator's physical entrance into our troubled world cannot be described without wild words. Let us return to the story of the One born in the stable in Bethlehem.

We cannot truly appreciate the incredible good news of the resurrection unless we first look at the ghastly death from which Jesus was resurrected. Jesus of Nazareth, both divine Creator and real human being, was nailed to a wooden cross between two common criminals, and he died an agonizing death. He was condemned by his religious leaders and betrayed by one disciple; another of his most trusted followers denied knowing him, and the other disciples fled, fearing for their own lives. Jesus was taken from the cross and buried in the tomb of Joseph of Arimathea. And then, three days later, he rose triumphant from the dead, a human being and yet radiating new divine light and power.

After a close brush with death, Henri Nouwen wrote that dying can be the most important act of living: "It involves a choice: to bind others with guilt or set them free with gratitude. This choice is a choice between a death that gives life or a death that kills."[2] Jesus' death perfectly demonstrates the truth of Nouwen's reflection. The dignity and composure, the forgiveness and honesty with which this human being died so impressed the Roman centurion in charge of the execution that he exclaimed, "Truly this man was God's son."[3] Even the pagan centurion sensed the divine holiness of this man. Jesus died as he had lived, in a way that hints that his death might not have been in vain.

Jesus spoke only seven times from the cross. The first two times he uttered words of forgiveness. Looking out on those who had crucified him and at spectators who came to watch him die, he said: "Father, forgive them, for they do not know what they are doing."[4] And then, turning his head toward one crucified with him who had defended him, he said: "Truly I tell you, today you will be with me in Paradise."

Then Jesus' sheer humanness broke forth in a cry of pure physical pain, the agony of a person bleeding to death—a cry so often heard from the wounded on battlefields: "I am thirsty." In the words that followed, Jesus expressed the pain of emotional and spiritual dereliction, the pain of hopelessness that so many of us feel in our broken world: "My God, my God, why have you forsaken me?" Then, looking down from the cross, Jesus saw his mother weeping and his beloved disciple John standing beside her. He spoke quietly: "Woman, here is your son." The words that followed were to his friend: "Here is your mother." In this simple affirmation of his human attachments, he sanctified our need for one another and the deep mystery of human love.

Jesus realized that death was about to engulf him. He spoke two last times as a mortal human being, and both times his passionate words suggest a resolution to his emotional pain—and even a flicker of hope. Quietly, almost to himself, he said: "It is finished." The Greek word that appears in the biblical text does not mean merely that the end of life had come, but rather that the task was completed. The life and work that began in the Creator's birth in a stable had come to completion, fulfillment, and fruition. Jesus' head fell on his chest and with his last breath he cried out to the One he called Abba: "Father, into your hands I commend my spirit." Jesus died. The Creator who entered our world knew existentially the agony and mystery of human suffering and death. The spirit of creative love had become one of us and was with us in our most profound questioning and misery.

Jesus' Resurrection

Jesus was crucified on Friday. Saturday, the Sabbath, was a black and agonizing day for Jesus' followers. They sat without words in a locked room in utter despair. They had lost everything, all hope. They feared that the Temple guard might come after them at any moment. Only the women were not crushed in despair; they were preparing the spices and cloth necessary for embalming Jesus' body. As dawn was breaking on Sunday, the first day of the Jewish week, the women took all the supplies needed for their painful task and started toward the tomb. They were discussing the problem of moving the heavy stone placed in front of the entrance to the sepulcher. But when the tomb came into view, they saw that the stone already had been rolled aside. Several women hurried forward and entered the crypt; there sat a luminous figure who looked like a young man dressed in white. The angel told them Jesus was not there, he had been raised from the dead.

The women were frightened—as all the others in our story had been when encountering a divine messenger. Then this strange being spoke again to them, and it was as if the Holy One were talking directly to them. The angel's words turned their lives upside down: "Do not be alarmed; you are looking for Jesus of Nazareth, who was crucified. He has been raised; he is not here. Look, there is the place they laid him. But go, tell his disciples and Peter that he is going ahead of you to Galilee; there you will see him, just as he told you."[5] The presence of this angelic being and the idea that a man who died from the torture of crucifixion could rise again were too much for them. They fled in fear and confusion. The world, apparently, was not as it previously had seemed. Evil did not always conquer—even Rome and the emperor were not the final power—and this Jesus, their friend, was even more than they had dreamed he might be. He had overcome death.

Only Mary Magdalene remained behind. They had killed the One who had saved her life who was her most faithful friend, and who had integrated her into the fellowship of women who had supported Jesus and his disciples in their mission. Now someone had stolen his body. It was more than she could bear. She sat down on a rock not far from the tomb and dissolved in tears. After a minute she got up and went to find Peter and the beloved disciple.

The other women gradually came to their senses and went to where the disciples were hiding; they too were afraid the Temple guard would seek to arrest them. The women delivered the angel's message to the despairing disciples. The men did not take the women seriously; humans need to be touched by the Holy to believe its reality—it is hard to believe from another what we have not directly experienced.

These women left, and Mary then came to the disciples' refuge and pleaded quietly with Peter and the beloved disciple to come and see what had happened. Peter and John were strangely moved by Mary and her story. They rushed out of the room and ran toward the tomb. John arrived at the tomb first, but he waited for Peter, who ran right up to the tomb, bent over, and entered it; Peter saw the cloth that had been around Jesus' head, rolled up and in a different place than the shroud, which lay just as if Jesus' body had evaporated. Peter, deeply puzzled by what he saw, came out. Then the beloved disciple entered. He saw that the absence of Jesus' body was not the work of grave robbers. A chill passed through him, and he realized Jesus had arisen and was alive. Slowly John and Peter walked down the hill, and when they reached the other disciples, they described what they had found. John expressed his belief, but none of the others took him seriously.

Mary Magdalene lingered near the tomb after the men went back to join their comrades. She wandered back, bent over, and looked into the tomb; even through her tears, she was dazzled by the brilliance of the two angels she saw inside. One angel asked her a question that struck into her heart and produced an even greater flood of tears: "Woman, why are you weeping?" Her answer seemed to say: Why can't you understand? "They have taken away my Lord, and I do not know where they have laid him." As she said this, she turned around and through her tears she caught a blurred sight of someone standing behind her. The person spoke to her the same ridiculous words the angel had used: "Woman, why are you weeping?" Mary thought it must be the gardener, and she asked politely: "Sir, if you have taken him away, tell me where he is, and I will take him away." Then Jesus called her by name: "Mary." Her ears heard and knew what her eyes had not seen. Mary called out "Rabbouni," fell at Jesus' feet, and threw her arms around his legs. Jesus said to her: "Stop clinging to me, because I have not yet ascended to the Father."[6] Then Jesus disappeared as unexpectedly as he had come.

In this brief encounter, Mary was carried from the deepest agony to the very glory of heaven. She skipped as she ran down the hill, picking the lilies and throwing them into the air; she was singing and laughing. *Jesus was alive. All was well with the world. The reign of the Holy One was real.* When she told her story to the disciples, only John, the beloved disciple believed her. (So often in my own deepest darkness, when I am open and seek his presence, I find the Risen Christ is there—waiting to lighten my darkness and lift me up. Often it seems to me that my most difficult crosses force me to seek and find the Light, which enables me to go on. Seldom do we find transformation unless we have dealt with evil and darkness.)

That very same Sunday morning, two of Jesus' friends were returning home to Emmaus from Jerusalem. They were talking about the horrible death their master had endured on Friday. They had been hoping Jesus would usher in the reign of heaven at the Passover. Jesus and their hopes had been destroyed, but they were going back home to take up their lives again; they would fight on through their despair. A stranger fell into step with them and asked them what they were discussing that made them so dejected. After they shared their heartbreaking pain about Jesus, the stranger began to explain the scriptures to them; he told them how the Messiah had to die and rise again, had to suffer and be raised up. When they reached their home, the stranger started to go on, but they pressed him to stay with them and have supper; he entered the house with them and sat at the table. Cleopas and his friend brought out bread and wine. The stranger took the bread and broke it, and their eyes were opened; they knew it was Jesus resurrected. Then Jesus disappeared.

These two men looked at one another in utter amazement. Cleopas exclaimed: "How could this be? But look, the loaf is broken on the plate." They could not wait to tell the disciples in Jerusalem. They left the bread and wine sitting on the table and *ran* the five or six miles back to Jerusalem. They pounded on the door where the disciples were staying. When the door was finally opened, they found a transformed group of the disciples and their companions, who cried out: "The Lord is risen indeed, and he has appeared to Simon." The men from Emmaus described their encounter with Jesus on the road and in the breaking of bread.

While they were still speaking, Jesus appeared in their midst and said, "Peace be with you." Some disciples who had not met the risen Jesus were frightened and acted as though they were seeing a ghost. Jesus asked them why they were so upset. He asked them to look at his hands and his feet and to touch him in order to realize he had human flesh and bones. Then he shared a meal with them and ate a piece of broiled fish. It was still difficult for the disciples to trust what they had experienced and to believe in the love Jesus expressed in his return to them.[7] They wondered why he would want to come to Peter, who had denied him, and to the disciples who had fled in terror when the Temple guard arrested Jesus.

Easter was not just one day; Jesus continued to appear to his friends for forty days, and various people encountered him at different times. The disciple Thomas had not been with the eleven when Jesus first appeared to them, and he believed his friends were suffering a group delusion created by wishful thinking. Thomas put it very bluntly, "Unless I see the mark of the nails in his hands, and put my finger in the mark of the nails and my hand in his side, I will not believe." But a week later, when Thomas was with the disciples, Jesus appeared to them all and greeted them, "Peace be with you." Then he turned to Thomas, "Put your finger here and see my hands. Reach out your hand and put it in my side. Do not doubt but believe." Thomas fell on his knees and exclaimed, "My Lord and my God." Jesus replied, "Have you believed me because you have seen me? Blessed are those who have not seen and yet have come to believe."[8]

Jesus appeared to his followers again a few weeks later. Since they had no sense of vocation, no realization that they should undertake a new calling, they were still working as fishermen. They did not yet understand what the resurrection of Jesus meant to them and what they should do about it. The seven of them had cast their fishing nets all through the night and had caught nothing. Just after dawn Jesus appeared on the shore and called out to them, asking if they had caught anything. When they replied that they had not, Jesus told them to cast their net on the right side of the boat. When they did so, they caught a huge number of large fish. The disciple whom Jesus loved realized it was the Lord and told Peter that it was Jesus. Peter was so excited he jumped into the water and waded ashore. He was thinking of the first great catch of fish after Jesus had called him to follow him. When the other disciples joined Peter, they found that Jesus had prepared a fire to toast bread and broil the fish. When they had finished eating, Jesus took Peter aside and asked him three times if he loved him. Each time that Peter told Jesus he loved him, Jesus gave Peter a command: "Feed my lambs. Tend my sheep. Feed my sheep."[9] Peter understood the evidence of his love for Jesus would be how he loved and led others. Peter began by sharing the commands with all Jesus' followers; the rest then understood their call as well.

A Joyful Parting

For more than a month Jesus appeared to his disciples and his family and friends. The resurrected Jesus appeared suddenly and then disappeared in the same way. The risen Jesus was training his followers to be constantly aware of his presence, to be spiritually on tiptoe. These strange comings and goings fostered this kind of awareness. Since they never knew when he would be present with them or in their midst, they came to think of his being with them in every conversation, at every meeting with a friend or enemy, accompanying their every thought. They became spiritually open to his presence. They came to rely on their spiritual experience of Jesus in addition to their physical sense. These meetings occurred until his followers were utterly convinced of his resurrection and of his never-failing presence.

Describing an overwhelming, life-changing spiritual experience is always difficult. Modern Western languages are particularly poor in this regard. The last meeting with the risen Jesus, the Christ, was such an experience, and no description of it is entirely adequate. To some it appeared as though he stepped into a cloud and disappeared. In Jewish thought, the cloud was understood as the way Yahweh often appeared to human beings. To others there was a blazing spiritual light into which Jesus stepped and disappeared; to others he stepped into another dimension and could not be seen by human eyes. Since heaven was considered at that time to be above the earth, some witnesses had the feeling he had risen into heaven.

Each time I read the gospel story I find something I had missed before. The strangest part of Jesus' final physical departure was not the way the disciples experienced his leaving but the way they reacted to it. Although they had lost the physical presence of One whom they had come to love more than life itself, they nonetheless returned to Jerusalem with *great joy* and remained in prayer and praise waiting for the gift that Jesus had promised to give. Ordinarily we expect people to feel great sadness when they lose their leader and friend. When Elijah, for example, was carried off to heaven, into the presence of Yahweh, Elisha—in a typical Hebrew expression of profound grief—ripped apart his clothes.

Jesus' story is different, however; Jesus is the only great hero in history for whom no eulogy has ever been written and for whom no dirge ultimately was sung. Indeed, Jesus' followers' very lack of sadness is the key to understanding the significance of Jesus' ascension—that time when his risen body was no longer visible to his friends and family. They were not sad because they had lost nothing. Jesus the Christ was a present reality for them. The early Christians never spoke of remembering Jesus; he was constantly with them as a real spiritual presence.

Had a modern physicist like the nuclear physicist-theologian John Polkinghorne been present, he might have expressed himself in a different way. He might have described it as the Holy One making eternal the flesh with which he had merged in the womb of Mary as a baby in the stable in

Bethlehem. Or a poet could have used the words of Howard Chandler
Robbins's hymn:

> And have the bright immensities
>   Received our risen Lord,
> Where light-years frame the Pleiedes
>   And point Orion's sword?
> Do flaming suns his footsteps trace
>   Through corridors sublime,
> The Lord of interstellar space
>   And Conqueror of time?

> The heav'n that hides him from our sight
>   Knows neither near or far:
> An altar candle sheds its light
>   As surely as a star;
> And where his loving people meet
>   To share the gift divine,
> There stands he with unhurrying feet;
>   There heav'nly splendors shine.[10]

A New Era Begins

The last words that Jesus spoke to his disciples before he disappeared
from their physical sight were an answer to their question, "When will you
restore the kingdom to Israel?" Jesus told them that it was not for them to
know such things, and he went on, "But you will receive power when the
Holy Spirit has come upon you; and you will be my witnesses in Jerusalem,
in all Judea and Samaria, and to the ends of the earth." Then he vanished
in a blaze of glory. The disciples were dazed by this experience, and some
of them were gazing into the sky; then suddenly, two of the Holy One's
messengers stood beside them telling them that they should stop staring
into the sky and go back to Jerusalem and wait. Jesus would return in the
same way he had left them.[11]

Joyfully, this group of disciples went back to the large upper room
where Jesus' followers had been staying, the place where they had had
their last supper together. There the disciples, Mary the mother of Jesus,
and Jesus' brothers spent most of their days together. Each time they ate
together and broke bread, Jesus seemed very close to them. They remembered the last meal they had had together, and they gave thanks for Jesus'
resurrection and life. These meals began with a thanksgiving not only for
the food they were about to eat but also for the incredible love of Jesus
who had revealed to them the infinite mercy and creativity of Abba, the
Holy One of Israel. During this period, the disciples felt the loss of Judas
and selected one of their fellowship to take his place.

Day after day they met together, broke bread together, and waited faithfully. They had discovered that Jesus was true to his promises, even to rising from the dead. They did not know what they were waiting for, but Jesus had promised an advocate, the Holy Spirit, a defender, a Paraclete for them. They had no idea in what form the empowering spirit of the Holy One would come, but they waited and trusted. Then suddenly one day a rushing mighty wind swept through the upper guest chamber in which they had been praying and praising Abba. (The word for "wind" is the same as the word for "spirit" in both Hebrew and Greek.) The Holy One had come in a blast of wind, much like the whirlwind out of which Yahweh spoke to Job. Then, looking at one another, the disciples saw tongues of fire, halos of fire resting on one another. This was their spiritual coronation. They were visibly crowned with light as the wind of spirit swirled around them, and they spoke in strange tongues and realized they could understand the meaning of what others were speaking.[12]

Those present were empowered in a new way. Their call and task became clearer to them. They continued to meet together in Jerusalem, but they also went out through Judea; they proclaimed the good news of the resurrected Christ and of the love of God that Jesus had lived out for them. They also healed the physically and mentally sick. Soon one of the persecutors of the new fellowship of Christians met Christ on the Damascus road; he was transformed, and in time he became one of the most articulate teachers to the Gentiles. Peter was called by Cornelius's vision and by his own vision to understand that the Gentiles as well as the Jews could be transformed by the contagious power that the disciples passed on to others; those who were touched by this message and spirit in turn passed the love and joy and confidence, the courage and power, on to others. Within forty years there were churches, fellowships of Christians, in all the major cities of the Roman Empire. As noted earlier, this same kind of vital spiritual life has continued throughout the years. When the power and life of this Holy Spirit has burned vividly in human lives, we have called these people saints. And there are millions more saints than those canonized by the churches; in the last sentence of *Middlemarch*, George Eliot makes this point well: "That all is not so ill with you and me as it might have is largely due to those who lived hidden lives and now rest in unvisited graves." All this began with—and would not have been possible without—the incarnation, the birth of Jesus in the stable in Bethlehem. No wonder the angels sang that night.

The Meaning of
These Strange Events

The resurrection experience means far more than the return of life to a dead body. The Gospels describe several instances when Jesus and the disciples raised the dead to life; these events are startling but not earth-shaking. A dead body did come to life, but far more happened at Jesus' resurrection. The Greek word usually translated "resurrection" (*anastasis*) is derived from a verb meaning "to draw up, to rise, to rise from, to overcome, to be transformed, to come to new life, or to partake in divine or eternal life." John Sanford in his *Mystical Christianity* has written that the Greek word "is to be understood not only in the narrower sense of a restoration from death to life, but also in the broader sense of a general spiritual awakening and renewal of life in all its dimensions."[13]

The first few verses of the Gospel of John link together the birth of Jesus (incarnation, the emptying of the divine Creator into human flesh), Jesus' life and teaching, his crucifixion, his resurrection, ascension and the pouring out of the Holy Spirit. They are all part of the divine action, one cosmic drama:

> In the beginning was the Word [logos], and the Word was with God, and the Word was God. . . . What has come into being in him was life, and the life was the light of all people. The light shines in the darkness, and the darkness did not overcome it. . . . And the Word became flesh and lived among us, and we have seen his glory, the glory as of a father's only son, full of grace and truth. . . . From his fullness we have all received, grace upon grace.[14]

The Gospel of John gives us the clue to the meaning of the resurrection of Jesus. Jesus did indeed return to life in a glorified body, in which he appeared to many of his disciples and friends. The disciples also underwent the ineffable experience of Jesus' ascension, in which Jesus' full identity with the Holy One was revealed to them. They had an overwhelming encounter with the Holy Spirit on the Jewish feast of Pentecost, a harvest festival. (This was truly a spiritual harvest!) So the resurrection is a three-part event, which took place dramatically and has continued through the years since it first occurred.

The resurrection was like the first gigantic and mysterious explosion of light with which the Creator began the creation of our universe. That event of fifteen billion years ago was the beginning of our universe, which finally resulted in the creation of human beings who were capable of knowing and responding to the loving Creator. Then, in Bethlehem, Jesus the Creator entered that created physical universe to reveal the nature of the Holy One. Jesus grew up and began a ministry, and he healed, taught, proclaimed that the reign of God was a present reality; in his healing and love he manifested the love of the Creator; he was then betrayed and crucified, and he died. But Jesus the Christ sprang forth in a burst of spiritual light—sprang forth from the grasp of death, darkness, and evil. He appeared to his disciples, manifested his oneness with the Holy One, the Creator, in the ascension, and then empowered his faithful followers with the Holy Spirit.

Luminous angels announced to frightened women the consummation of the drama, the same angels that sang of peace and joy and love to the frightened shepherds. Indeed, anyone who is not a little frightened by the resurrection of Jesus has not truly understood it. Most of the disciples also were frightened at first when Jesus appeared to them in a mysterious spiritual-physical body; this new reality could be touched and felt and could consume fish and bread, but at the same time could pass through stout wooden doors. Today some people find these stories incredible, and assume they are mere fiction; but those who are doubtful about this glorified body, paradoxically both spirit and flesh, ought to meditate on the paradox that a "physical particle" of light also acts like a wave. John Polkinghorne argues that the increasing mystery of physical matter is revealed to any who would trouble themselves to study quantum mechanics; the mystery of Jesus brings us into the heart of the mystery of the universe. The resurrection of Jesus also asserts that death and evil have been defeated and have no final power over this world or the women and men within it, in spite of what we see within ourselves or in the world around us. We human beings can be resurrected with Jesus and share in the ever-expanding and limitless potentiality of eternal life; you and I can become children and partners in the reign of the Holy One now and eternally.

We cannot catch the full, immense, and stunning meaning of the last act of the Creator's divine drama unless we set it against the backdrop of human depravity and the agony of Good Friday. If human beings can be redeemed from that, we can be resurrected from anything. I am not naively claiming, however, that all is now well in the world. When we look at the continuing ghastly conflicts on all levels of the outer world, it becomes perfectly obvious to us that all is *not* well. When we look at the Herod, the innkeeper, or the Judas in each of us, we cannot say that "all is well" in the depth of ourselves.

The birth-life-crucifixion-resurrection-ascension-bestowing the Holy Spirit are parts of one drama. The divine action helps us dare to look at the worst in ourselves and in the world *and at the best within us human beings and at the best in our world.* As we gaze at the total picture of creation, we can begin to realize that although there is darkness, there is hope for us all. Darkness has tried to put out the Light, but from an eternal perspective, the Light is never extinguished. In the last chapter of *Mystical Christianity*, John Sanford shows clearly that the essential message of the cross and *resurrection* "is the most hopeful statement in the spiritual lore of humankind." In the birth of Jesus we perceive intimations of this truth; in the last act of the divine play we are shown dramatically the dazzling victory of holy love and its continuous presence with us now.

Jesus who was crucified did not remain dead. He was resurrected; this historical event proclaims the incredible good news that the Creator shared in our humanity to enable us to share in the divine life and resurrection. Several of the early, heroic Christians wrote: "The Divine became what we are that we may become what the Divine is." We can find new life in the risen Christ, an eternal life with power, love, and courage.

13

Letting Christ into Our Lives

Christmas tells us that the loving Creator wanted to enter our world and our individual lives. Easter announces that this Holy One loves us so much that Jesus was willing to die on a cross and rise again to show the depth of his love for us and to bring us into the orbit of divine love. Pentecost tells us that the Holy Spirit of the incarnate Christ wishes to dwell in each of us. How can we open our lives to this Holy One, who wants to relate to us and bring us to fulfillment not only in this mortal life but in eternity? For forty years I have been meditating, thinking, discussing, listening, and reading the Bible and the accounts of the lives of Jesus' most sincere friends in order to answer this question. The basic point of this book is lost if I do not conclude with some suggestions about how we can allow our lives to be directed by the incredibly loving Christ.[1]

One very important insight has come to me in these years: We human beings are capable of closing the doors of our lives to the knocking of divine love. The Creator is infinitely wise—both in the creation of this planet in which humans can grow enough to relate to divine love and in the treatment of human beings themselves. The Holy One revealed by Jesus Christ loves us and wants our love in return. For love to be real, however, we have to be free to love or not to love; we cannot be mere automatons. So the Divine has given us freedom and power. We can ignore and shut out the loving Creator.

Two common human practices can effectively keep the Holy Spirit from meddling in our lives. First of all, we can keep so busy that we never stop to think about the meaning of life, of the mystery of our lives, the mystery of the universe. We can avoid the meaning of our lives by never stopping to pause and reflect. We can even be so busy with religious affairs that we have no time to relate to the risen Jesus. The adage is true: Busyness is not of the devil; busyness is the devil. We also can avoid the loving Creator in a second way: We can be so absorbed in outer material things—in clothes, entertainment, human fame, delicious food, our power or money—that we ignore the *fact* that there is a spiritual world as well as a material world. If we do this, we never lift our eyes above the earthly horizon; we are caught in the Western illusion that only the physical, material world is real.

If that materialistic point of view is true, the entire biblical story is false; indeed, all the great religions of humankind are nonsense. Several years ago I was lecturing in Singapore to a group of clergy whose ethnic roots were in China and India. When I tried to explain to them how many people in Western Europe and America have been brainwashed into an exclusively materialistic world view, they could hardly believe it. For them the spiritual world is probably more real and important than the physical one. They *know* the reality of the spiritual domain, both good and evil.

Once we have come to the conclusion that there is more to seek than merely material things, then we need to set aside a time daily to pause and reflect. We need fifteen to thirty minutes of quiet and silence in which we can reflect on our lives and their meaning from the vantage point of eternity. In quiet we can come to an inner honesty and self-confrontation. It is easy to become so busy or occupied in outer tasks that we avoid ourselves and the ultimate issues and how they relate to us. Without times of silence, prayer, and meditation, we can avoid the divine lover, the reality of the Holy, that Jesus revealed to us. I find I need daily times of quiet if I am to see clearly who I am, what I wish to become, and what my priorities really are.

Keeping a daily diary or religious journal is essential for me. Without it I do not stop and record my experience of the Divine, my failings, my lack of caring for others, my busyness, my new insights. Many people have told me that as soon as they began to keep a religious journal, their spiritual lives became more and more real; they had more sense of the presence and direction of the Christ. When they began to record their dreams, visions, and religious intuitions, they found that the dreams and visions of the first Christmas and Easter and those described in the Acts of the Apostles were being repeated in their lives. The Holy Spirit was guiding them as soon as they stopped and listened. As I become quiet and listen to the knocking on the doorway of my soul and open the door, I find the risen Jesus present to deal with the difficulties and complexities of my life as well as to feed my soul.

In order to pray we need to know the One to whom we are praying. At this point I need a religious tradition. Those who make their own religion are usually the most naive and deluded of all people. Jesus had a religious tradition, and he made only a few changes in it; he added a few insights into the loving nature of the Creator he called "Abba." John Sanford tells of his exploration of various religious traditions, and I have had the same experience. I too have looked at all the major, traditional religions of humankind, and many of the new ones, and I find that the Holy One revealed by Jesus of Nazareth gives me the best and most hopeful picture of the divine reality. As I read this story of Jesus and his disciples and meditate on it, I learn more about myself and the Holy than I do from any other religious tradition.

Yet I cannot fully understand Jesus unless I know his tradition and scripture, the Old Testament. As I have meditated on and carefully studied the Christmas story for this writing, I have learned much that I never knew before about Jesus' religious tradition. As I have read the history of the church, I also have learned more about the reality of the loving Creator. I have discovered, furthermore, that I need fellowship with other people who have lived with the story of Jesus and who know the book that was scripture for him. Such fellowship helps me see more and more clearly the dazzling reality of the loving Creator.

Prayer is not so much asking for what we wish from the Divine as it is fellowship with the Holy One who wants our presence far more than we want the Holy One's presence. The One who suffered and rose from the dead also is able to lift me up out of my darkness and despair when my life seems hopeless. The Holy One pours the healing oil of love on me. But prayer is for good times as well as bad: When all is going well, relating to the Risen One is pure joy. There is no single prescription for how to pray. Some people find the prayer of inward silence enough; they need no images—only the simple sense of presence (often called the dazzling darkness). This is the way of many Quakers and Christian contemplatives, and of those in some other religious traditions.

In my prayer life many biblical images are healing and encouraging to me. Mary and Joseph, the shepherds, the baby in the manger, the Magi, the Old Testament prophets, the Savior on the cross dying for us, that strange postresurrection body—the list is endless. Such images assist some of us in relating to the loving One who created the universe so that we might have fellowship with this ineffable Creator who is reaching out to us. Ignatius of Loyola, for example, used this way of prayer. Our human capacity to know is infinitely greater than we ordinarily realize. We can pray in images, the language of imagination (which speaks also in dreams and visions, literature, and mythology). Indeed, throughout these pages we have been exploring the coming of the Creator into our troubled world by letting our imaginations play over the Bible story of Christmas.

On the religious journey, we need not only a tradition and a church or fellowship of which we are part but also special companions with whom we can share our goals, our visions of eternity, our experiences of the Divine. We especially need their understanding when the road is difficult or when we seem to be cut off from our spiritual light. Without these companions on the inner way, it is very hard to understand ourselves and make the most of the human potentiality we have been given. One chief purpose of any religious fellowship is to provide such companions. Furthermore, if we are to be good companions on this journey, we need to know something of the depth and complexity of the human psyche or soul—*psychology* in the true meaning of that word.

How can we continue in relation with divine love unless we share the love poured out on us with others—even with people we may not like? In the same way that the Creator sends rain on the just and the unjust, we need to love even those who may be as unworthy of our love as we are of the Christ's love, the Creator's love. How difficult it is to cease our critical judging of others, for so often our judging is a projection of our *own* faults on others. Most problems in our world arise from vengeance, greed, and hatred, from people who have been abused by receiving too little love and too much criticism. The child who has not been truly loved by parents or others is an abused child who often grows up to abuse others.

We cannot take on all the injustice and need in the world, but we can look honestly at the vast human need for food, support, and caring and find in our quiet time specifically what the risen Christ would have us do. In addition, in order to love at all, we need to love ourselves. I can do this only when I look at the Christ who has loved me with all my faults. I am denying and rejecting the risen Jesus if I do not try to love myself, one of those for whom he died. As I accept my own failing, I am more likely to accept the faults of others. I am no longer in a position to judge other people.

Our caring is needed in so many places we need a constant supply of divine love if we are to have the reservoir of caring that we need. We are called to love our families and friends, the stranger and the enemy, the forgotten and the starving, the sick and dying, those in prison, the lonely, and the depressed. Again the list is endless, and we need divine guidance to become the effective instruments of divine love. Mother Teresa is one who heard a call and followed it—and has drawn thousands to serve with her. The more the Christ dwells within us, the more we too can be instruments of creative, healing love. Our growth into the fullness of our potential as children of the divine Creator can be measured more accurately by the healing love and caring we give to others than by any other standard. This can be frightening when we see how often we fail.

One of the best responses to our very reasonable fear of inadequacy, of being unable to love truly and selflessly, is found in the words of Father Zosima in Dostoyevski's *The Brothers Karamazov*:

> Never be afraid of your petty selfishness when you try to achieve love, and don't be too alarmed if you act badly on occasion. I'm sorry I cannot

tell you anything more reassuring. A true act of love, unlike imaginary love, is hard and forbidding. Imaginary love yearns for an immediate heroic act that is achieved quickly and seen by everyone. People may actually reach a point where they are willing to sacrifice their lives, as long as the ordeal doesn't take too long, is quickly over—just like on the stage, with the public watching and admiring. A true act of love, on the other hand, requires hard work and patience, and, for some, it is a whole way of life. But I predict that at the very moment when you see despairingly that, despite all your efforts, you have not only failed to come closer to your goal but, indeed, seem even farther from it than ever—at that very moment, you will have achieved your goal and will recognize the miraculous power of our Lord, who has always loved you and has secretly guided you all along.[2]

A Prayer for Christmas Eve
and Christmas Day
and for Each Day of the Year

One Christmas many years ago I knew that as a preacher I had to present a message, but no message came to me; a prayer, however, came into my heart and mind. I shared it then, and I share it now with you, my readers.

Oh, divine Creator, you who exist beyond our physical universe and within it and even within my heart; Jesus said that the kingdom of heaven is within us. You created the heavens and stars and the infinite complexity of our material world; you are the source and foundation of all things. We are given courage to turn to you not because of our virtue, but because you came to us many years ago in a stable on a bright chilly night.

Were it not for your coming to us with such humility and grace, I doubt if I would be able to turn to you now. For some reason beyond my understanding, you cherish us human beings and you sent your Son, your creative being, to Mary and to Joseph and to the world. As I turn to you, Abba, I humbly ask one thing only: that you send the infant Christ to be born in my heart. Let him grow there to bring peace, joy, strength and courage, understanding and patience, love and gratitude. Once I experience these gifts, I can share them with all those around me.

Abba, I have tried to bring my confused life into order, and I find I cannot do it without your help. My life is torn and divided like the world into which the Christ child came. There are parts of me like Herod who would destroy this divine child. There are parts of me like the Romans who would rule my life for their advantage. There are parts of me that are broken and sick, in bondage and prison, just as there were in the world in which Jesus came. I have tried again and again to bring harmony, peace, and love into my soul, but where joy might abide, there is often sorrow; where I should find peace, I see conflict; where I would like to find strength and courage, I discover cowardice and weakness; where I would like to see love and gratitude, there is anger and selfishness; where I look for humility and simplicity, I see pride.

I do not like what I find within me as it mirrors the world around me. Try as hard as I can, I cannot change myself without your help. Abba, send the Christ child into my heart and let his spirit grow in me. His spirit can knit the tattered, raveled edges of my soul. Only the indwelling Christ can reconcile the conflicting, antagonistic forces that war in our world and within us. Only he can make the lion lie down with the lamb.

Abba, send your Son into my heart, that he may not only be born there but also grow and mature and take over the direction of my life. May your love make of me something of value and worth, someone in whom you can rejoice. May the stable of my soul be transformed and become a temple filled with your Spirit. May my soul be transformed and become a beacon, shedding light in the midst of a dark and troubled world. Oh, risen Jesus, I pray this in your name, you who humbled yourself to be born of a virgin in a stable in an occupied country in order to show me the infinite mercy and love of the divine Creator.

Epilogue

Aurora Borealis

Aurora.
There in the sky, the wheel.
O, Ezekiel knew
and said,
"God."
There in the sky, the light,
O, the shepherds knew
and said,
"Angel."
There in the sky, the radiance.
O, do the people know
to say,
"Being"?

Borealis.
Like angels descending—
towers of light! drapieres of light!
ladders of light over our town:
God's messengers going up and down
over our fields on ladders of golden light—
energy pure as light streaming from the sun,
particles charged with the glory of God,
and the planet, reaching, touches radiance.
Suppose we could like particles be charged—

God in us as ions from the sun,
God in us as being, God in us as loving—
we could rise streaming God across the sky.
Then might we over our houses rise,
meeting as angels—hovering, shining,
greeting each other in reaching announcement of love:
love touching love in great arcs visible,
sheeting like curtains, like color rippling,
flaring from touch to touch, announcement of love
shining like towers, like angels wheeling.
Announcement of love—in us the Child:
luminous energy charged with God,
each of us afire, each of us shimmering;
neighbors running onto their porches to see
all of us shining and touching over the chimneys,
over the rooftops luminous radiant, announcing love.
All the way up, aurora touching heaven:
love touching love touching love touching angels.
Everywhere, everywhere over our houses,
arches and arcs of touching and flaring
love touching love touching angels.
Hands reaching, sight reaching, thought reaching,
leaping arcs, leaping light, constellations of gladness
standing over all our houses—great blue arcs—O Gabriel!
Aurora. Aurora Borealis.

—Nancy Evans Bush

Acknowledgments

Grateful acknowledgment is made to the following for permission to reproduce copyrighted materials:

Random House, Inc. for excerpts from W. H. Auden, *For The Time Being: A Christmas Oratorio* in *Religious Drama 1,* copyright 1957 by Meridian Books.

Doubleday & Co. for excerpt from Raymond Brown, *The Birth of the Messiah,* copyright 1977 and used by permission.

Nancy Evans Bush and the Asylum Hill Congregational Church, Hartford, Conn. for permission to reprint her poem *Aurora Borealis.*

Alison Curry for permission to reprint her article "Tolerance" in *Democracy in Action,* vol. 1, no. 7.

Bantam Books for excerpt from Fyodor Dostoyevski, *The Brothers Karamazov,* copyright 1970.

Harcourt, Brace & Co. for excerpts from T. S. Eliot, *Collected Poems 1909–1962,* copyright 1963.

HarperCollins for excerpt from Andrew M. Greeley, *The Mary Myth,* copyright 1977 by The Seabury Press.

Princeton University Press for excerpt from C. G. Jung, *Jung's Letters,* ed. Gerhard Adler and Aniela Jaffe, copyright 1973.

Augsburg Publishing House for excerpt from Pinchas Lapide, *The Resurrection of Jesus,* copyright 1983 and used by permission of Augsburg Fortress.

Crossroad Publishing Co. for excerpt from Henri Nouwen, *Beyond the Mirror,* copyright 1990.

Caryl Porter for permission to reprint her poem *Looking toward Christmas.*

Crossroad Publishing Co. for excerpts from John Sanford, *Mystical Christianity,* copyright 1993 and for excerpts from Morton Kelsey, *Afterlife,* copyright 1986, and *Tongue Speaking,* copyright 1981. Used with permission of the author.

The Church Pension Fund for hymns quoted from *The Hymnal of the Protestant Episcopal Church in the United States of America 1940.*

Notes

Chapter 1: The Mystery of Christmas

1. W. H. Auden, *For the Time Being: A Christmas Oratorio,* in *Religious Drama 1* (New York: Meridian Books, 1957), 67.

2. In *The Anthropic Cosmological Principle* (Oxford: Oxford University Press, 1989), John D. Barrow, a mathematical astronomer, and Frank J. Tipler, a mathematical physicist, present overwhelming evidence in great detail that the universe did not develop just by chance. The earth seems to have been created specifically to provide for the emergence of life. The universe was created so that it and its Creator could be observed. John Polkinghorne, formerly a professor of small-particle mathematics in the nucleus of the atom at Cambridge University and now an Anglican clergyperson and president of Queen's College, Cambridge, has drawn the theological implications of the mystery of creation revealed in modern physics in three remarkable books: *One World* (London: SPCK, 1986), *Science and Creation* (London: SPCK, 1988), *Science and Providence* (Boston: Shambahala, 1989). A popular presentation of the mystery of matter and the failure of mechanical and material explanations to account for the freedom that exists on the quantum level is contained in Paul Davies and John Gribbin, *The Matter Myth* (New York: Simon & Schuster, 1992).

3. John 1:14. Author's paraphrase.

4. See Philippians 2:5–7.

5. For over forty years I had preached and lectured on the events surrounding the birth of Jesus of Nazareth and on the Christian doctrine of incarnation—the idea that in Jesus, God became a human being. But I had never presented an entire conference on this subject until I was asked to do so at Tommy Tyson's Aquaduct Conference Center. As I prepared for this conference, I realized that my view of the truth and reality of the birth narratives was not shared by many liberal biblical critics. Many scholars pointed out the quite different traditions in the Gospels of Matthew and Luke. They also noted that

in the earliest gospel, Mark, there is no account of Jesus' birth at all and in the Gospel of John there is only a poetic account of the incarnation, but no reference to Mary, Joseph, or the other people so vividly described in Matthew and Luke. As I reflected on my seminary training, I realized that no attempt was made to give us an integrated or coherent picture of what really occurred at Jesus' birth *or* resurrection. The underlying reason for liberal critics' doubts about the historicity of the birth narrative is not the stated reason for this disbelief, but rather a lack of belief that a spiritual world can influence our physical world.

I discovered that one of the most respected and careful modern biblical critics, Raymond Brown, had written a detailed analysis of the birth narratives in his monumental study of the four chapters of the New Testament dealing with the birth and infancy of Jesus. In his book, *The Birth of the Messiah* (Garden City, N.Y.: Doubleday & Company, 1977), Brown examined every verse of the narratives and also a great number of the scholarly opinions pro and con regarding each passage. He concluded that the evidence and the consensus of scholarly opinion support the view that the basic biblical narrative can be accepted as history by responsible and clear-headed Christians.

Brown also reminds us that the four Gospels were written backward. They first recorded the details of Jesus' crucifixion, which made his resurrection so impressive. Then the Gospels recorded his healing ministry and made collections of Jesus' teachings. Finally, they described what they could learn about his birth. They are not biographies of Jesus, but proclamations of good news based on historical events. The earliest Christians lived in the euphoria of the resurrection experience; it was so much a part of the sacrificial lives of the first disciples that Mark spends only a few paragraphs of his breathless little book on the resurrection. In addition, experiences as earthshaking as the resurrection of Jesus were difficult to describe. Mark spends nearly one third of his imperfect Greek text describing the events that took place after Jesus entered Jerusalem for the last time; he describes Jesus' knowledge of what lay before him and then he tells of Jesus' condemnation and crucifixion. (Without the resurrection Mark's book is anything but good news.) Mark then added an account of the ministry of this remarkable man and provided graphic tableaus of his healing and teaching.

By the time Matthew and Luke came to write their expanded accounts of the good news about the incredible new life available in Jesus Christ, they incorporated an account of Jesus' birth. Matthew and Luke told the same basic story about Mary and Joseph, but with different complementary variations of detail. Brown has concluded that these evangelists believed the accounts of Jesus' birth were appropriate introductions to the career and significance of Jesus. As Brown puts it:

> To give them less value than other parts of the Gospels is to misread the mind of the evangelists for whom the infancy narratives were fitting vehicles of the message they wanted to convey. Indeed, from this point of view the infancy narratives are not an embarrassment but a masterpiece. Perhaps precisely because the material had been less fixed in the

course of apostolic preaching, the evangelists exercised greater freedom of composition. One is hard pressed to find elsewhere in the Gospels theology so succinctly and imaginatively presented.

Brown led me to the discovery that the first two chapters of these Gospels are "just as profoundly Christian and dramatically persuasive as the last two, the story of the passion and resurrection." The narratives are all of a piece (Brown, 38).

Matthew's and Luke's birth stories, furthermore, express the same essential message as the poetic theology of the first chapter of John's Gospel. John tells us in philosophical language how God came into the world in Jesus of Nazareth to draw the human race fully into the orbit of the divine mercy, grace, and love. Matthew and Luke give the concrete, temporal, dramatic details of how the Christ was born.

6. The dramatic presentation of the Christian story has had a long history. Eucharist can be seen as a reenactment of the last supper Jesus shared with his disciples before his crucifixion and resurrection. Mystery plays telling the whole story of Jesus were one of the most popular pastimes during the Middle Ages. People have come from all over the world to see the Oberammergau passion play. Two of the finest Christmas dramas were written in our century, one by W. H. Auden, "For the Time Being: A Christmas Oratorio," the other by Dorothy Sayers, *The Man Born to Be King*. Both of them present, with great power, a consecutive narrative of eternity entering time. They portray a view of the gospel story similar to the scholarly work of Raymond Brown. I follow and meditate on this essential narrative as I did in *Resurrection: Release from Oppression* (Mahweh, NJ: Paulist Press, 1985).

7. Phillips Brooks' hymn is found in *The Hymnal of the Protestant Episcopal Church* (New York: Seabury Press, 1943), no. 21.

Chapter 2: A Savior Is Born

1. In *The World's Religions*, Huston Smith classifies Judaism as one of the great world religions and presents an in-depth and sympathetic study of its genius (San Francisco: HarperCollins, 1991).

2. The translation of Luke 1:13–17, 18–20 is that of Raymond Brown, *The Birth of the Messiah* (Garden City, N.Y.: Doubleday & Company, 1977), 256–57, altered to avoid sexist language.

3. Luke 1:28, 30–38.

4. The definitive study of traditions concerning the virgin birth is also by Raymond E. Brown, *The Virginal Conception and Bodily Resurrection of Jesus* (New York: Paulist Press, 1973). What is possible? If one is caught in the materialistic world view and believes that we fully understand the nature of physical reality, then the virgin birth and the idea of incarnation is just plain absurdity. If, however, we understand something of quantum mechanics and the improbability of life's existing at all, it is possible to believe in providence in such an instance. John Polkinghorne's book *Science and Providence* (Boston: Shambahala, 1989) shows clearly that the Divine, as well as human beings, has

freedom. In John Barrows and Frank Tipler, *The Anthropic Cosmological Principle* (Oxford: Oxford University Press, 1989), 556–70, the improbability of human life's ever coming into existence is shown with great care. Barrows and Tipler sketch out three criteria for human life, and then they record ten improbable steps that have occurred to make human life possible on the planet Earth in our universe. We are far more wonderful than we ordinarily believe, and the world that supports our being is infinitely more complex than scientists of thirty to forty years ago ever imagined. Anyone who denies the virgin birth categorically without looking at modern science's evidence in support of providential events is simply naive.

5. W. H. Auden, *For the Time Being: A Christmas Oratorio* in *Religious Drama 1* (New York: Meridian Books, 1957), 27–28.

6. Matthew 1:20–21.

7. Auden, *For the Time Being*, 30.

8. Isaiah 7:14 as quoted in Matthew 1:23.

9. Some biblical critics are troubled by the differences between Matthew and Luke, but they need not reject the authenticity of both narratives because of these differences. The accounts are complementary and only contradictory in a few minor details. Even reporters writing about yesterday's events will select some details and leave others out. Historians must similarly be selective; several years ago I read five of the finest modern studies of the life of Julius Caesar. I could hardly believe these historians were all writing about the same person—a historical figure about whom a great deal of data is available. In short, every writer describing the past does it from his or her own point of view and usually for a particular readership.

Let us consider the situation in which Luke and Matthew were writing. Two authors with no knowledge of the other's work are trying to describe events that occurred eighty years before and for which few written documents existed. They had to rely on the traditions of the families and friends of the person whose birth they wish to describe. What is amazing is not that there are some differences in their accounts, but that the essential events are the same and the general focus and intent of both writers are almost identical. Could we do much better today faced with a similar task? History is not an exact science. Matthew was probably a Greek-speaking Jew with a knowledge of Hebrew. He was addressing a Christian community, most likely in Syria, that contained both Gentiles and Jews. His book was probably written to instruct new converts in the basic life and message of Jesus of Nazareth and in Christianity. Luke, on the other hand, was most likely a Greek-speaking Gentile converted by Paul or his followers. He wrote his book for Gentiles interested in the new religion; he used elegant Greek in the style of Hellenistic historians.

10. Translations of Luke 1:42–55 by Brown, *Birth of the Messiah*, 330–31.

11. Luke 1:68–79.

12. The quotations of Luke 2:10–12 and 14 are the author's translations of the Greek.

13. It is difficult for us to understand this belief that women are unclean during menstruation and for a period after the birth of a child. However, this tradition is found in many societies throughout our world. In *Sacrament of*

Sexuality (Rockport, Mass.: Element Books, 1991), 75–79, I have suggested that this may be related to the patriarchal fear of women. Mary and Joseph were obedient to the Law, but Jesus, being who he was, took another view of women and the Law. (The references in the Law to these rites are: Exodus 13:1, 11–16; Numbers 18:15–16; and Leviticus 12:1–8).

14. Translation of Luke 2:29–32 is by Brown, *Birth of the Messiah*, 435.

15. Luke 2:34–35. (NRSV)

16. Matthew 2:2. (author's translation)

17. Matthew 2:6.

18. Matthew 2:8.

19. Matthew 2:15.

20. Matthew 2:18.

21. From beginning to end the Christmas drama is guided by angelic messengers sent by the Holy One of Israel. Since the Enlightenment the subject of angels has been largely rejected, ignored or trivialized. Quite recently, a popular interest has risen concerning these divine messengers. *Time* magazine, Dec. 27, 1993, Vol. 152, no. 27, 54–65, reports surveys showing that sixty-nine percent of Americans believe in the existence of angels. The article explores the subject sympathetically and in depth and points out the awesome and terrifying aspect of a genuine encounter with the angelic. Milton and Rilke are quoted attesting to this awe that is part of this experience so well described in the New Testament birth narrative. As a pastor and counselor, I have heard many such experiences and have described them in several of my books.

Chapter 3: Mary

1. Luke 1:38.

2. W. H. Auden, *For the Time Being: A Christmas Oratorio* in *Religious Drama 1* (New York: Meridian Books, 1957), 24–25. A fine and sensitive portrayal of the annunciation also is provided by Sholem Asch in his novel, *Mary* (New York: Carroll & Graf Publishers, Inc., 1985), 35–39.

3. Luke 1:51–53.

4. Andrew Greeley, *The Sociology of the Paranormal: A Reconnaissance* (Beverly Hills, Calif.: Sage Publications, Inc., 1975), shows few people dare share their religious experiences in our society, particularly with religious professionals.

5. Luke 1:78–79.

6. Luke 2:34–35.

7. Trevor Hudson, a Methodist minister in South Africa, called my attention to the meditative role of Mary in the Christian story, and I quote his words.

8. Andrew Greeley, *The Mary Myth* (New York: The Seabury Press, 1977), 86.

9. Ibid., 196.

10. The stories of the trip to Elizabeth, the trips to Jerusalem, and the flight to Egypt are an imaginary expansion of the gospel accounts based on the geography of Palestine and Egypt and the life and customs of that time.

Chapter 4: Joseph the Carpenter

1. Raymond Brown, in *The Birth of the Messiah* (Garden City, N.Y.: Doubleday & Company, 1977), draws on the latest biblical research and on what we have learned from the Dead Sea Scrolls to give us a picture of what the ordinary religious person would have believed and done in Jesus' time. In addition, Harry Kemelman, *Conversations with Rabbi Small* (New York: Ballantine-Fawcett Crest, 1991), gives us a picture of contemporary Jewish belief and practice. The similarities between modern Jewish practice and that of Joseph's time are many. Most of us know too little about Jewish belief and practice in today's homes and synagogues to picture Joseph's religious life. Huston Smith in *The World's Religions* (San Francisco: HarperCollins, 1992) describes the Jewish religion as one of the world's great religions and gives an excellent understanding of its value and significance. When we allow our historical imagination to dwell on these facts, we can begin to see Joseph as a real person.

2. See Luke 10:30–36.

3. Matthew 1:20–21.

4. An excellent study of Jesus' language ability is presented in Joseph A. Fitzmyer, "Did Jesus Speak Greek," *Biblical Archaeological Review*, September-October, 1992. John Sanford came to the same conclusion by his continuous reading of the New Testament in Greek and by his respect for Jesus' almost incredible intelligence. Years of studying Jesus' sayings have convinced him of Jesus' wide language knowledge and wisdom.

5. The only serious modern interpretation of the importance and value of Joseph is by Leon Joseph Cardinal Suenens, *Cher Saint Joseph*, Edition F. I. A. T., Grovenplein 9, B-9940, Ertvelde, Belgium, 1993. Cardinal Suenens was one of the most important figures in Catholic renewal in Vatican Council II.

Chapter 5: Blessed Are the Shepherds
and the Stable

1. Luke 2:10–12

2. Luke 2:14; author's translation from the Greek.

3. Dreams of momentous events often take place in those who listen to them. Joseph and the Magi and many others listened to their dreams and visions. *The Book of Acts* and secular history are full of such experiences. See my book *God, Dreams and Revelation* (Minneapolis: Augsburg Fortress, 1991).

4. Matthew 11:28

5. See Luke 15:15–19.

6. Many of them had lice. Indeed, leprosy was rampant in Palestine because so many people had to live in unsanitary conditions. (We squeamish Westerners need to be reminded that cleanliness and holiness do not necessarily go hand in hand. According to legend, when St. Thomas à Becket was murdered in Canterbury Cathedral, a stream of lice was seen leaving his body, and people of that time were convinced this was evidence of his great holiness.

Lice and leprosy, signs of poverty and oppression, became signs of self-denial. Father Damien, the Belgian missionary, lived in squalid conditions among the abandoned lepers on Molokai and later contracted leprosy himself.)

7. See Matthew 20:1–16.

8. Many of the details about the shepherds are the result of study of actual conditions among the dispossessed in Palestine at the time of Jesus' birth. The conditions were similar to those of many people today.

9. This pamphlet, *Our Rag-Bone Hearts*, by Elizabeth O'Connor can be obtained through The Servant Leadership School, 1640 Columbia Road, N.W., Washington, D.C. 20009; (202) 328-1312.

Chapter 6: The Urchin

1. Stray animals are treated better in the Western world than stray children were at that time—or than they are in, for instance, Brazil today. (My wife and I were warned in Brazil to take off even our wedding rings, because desperate children and adults might knock us down; one gold ring could buy a month's supply of bread. We were told not to judge these people: they were hungry.)

2. Caryl Porter, *To Make All Things New* (Nashville: Broadman Press, 1987).

3. *Jung's Letters*, ed. Gerhard Adler and Aniela Jaffé (Princeton: Princeton University Press, 1973), 1:377. I have discussed the healing power of genuine religious experience in depth in *Psychology, Medicine and Healing* (San Francisco: Harper & Row, 1988).

4. This story of Jung is recorded in Aniela Jaffé, *From the Life and Work of C. G. Jung* (New York: Harper & Row, 1971). One of Laurens van der Post's finest stories, "Christmas Morning," tells a similar story. The story is found in van der Post's *The Seed and the Sower* (London: The Hogarth Press, 1974), 43–182.

5. John Shea, *Starlight: Beholding the Christmas Miracle All Year Long* (New York: Crossroads Publishing Company, 1992).

Chapter 7: The Innkeeper

1. The Greek word in Luke 2:7, *kataluma*, often translated "inn," has several meanings. It can be a dining room or a lodging set aside for guests. The upper room or guest chamber in which the disciples ate with Jesus, Luke 22:11, may well have been the same place the apostles and the women followers of Jesus received the gift of the Spirit at Pentecost. The verb related to this word is used in Luke 9:12 where it means "to find a place to spend the night." The word's literal meaning is "to unharness the pack animals." See *A Greek-English Lexicon of the New Testament and Other Early Christian Literature*, ed. by W. F. Arndt and F. W. Gingrich, (Chicago: University of Chicago Press, 1952).

2. Information about this program can be obtained from Don Mclanen, The Church of the Saviour, The Festival Center, 1640 Columbia Road, N. W., Washington, D.C. 20009; (202) 328-7312.

Chapter 8: A Third Road to Bethlehem

1. A full, scholarly account of the Magi is found in Raymond Brown, *The Birth of the Messiah* (Garden City, N.Y.: Doubleday & Company, 1977), 165–201. As Brown points out, many modern biblical critics have questioned the historicity of this story. Is the story probable? Under ordinary circumstances the answer would be no. But this was a special event of the Creator entering creation. We need not limit ourselves by what we think may be probable. When we examine the latest discoveries of modern physics and astronomy, we discover that the improbable indeed can occur. The mathematics of what occurred during the first few seconds of creation right up to the formation of a place like earth where life might develop are so improbable as to stagger the most imaginative mind. On top of this, the probabilities of the completion of the many stages necessary for the development of one-celled creatures into human beings capable of self-consciousness are astronomically small. In comparison, the probabilities of three Wise Men appearing on the scene of Jesus' birth are quite large. John Masefield has suggested that God created the earth for the joy he took in a rhyme and then filled it full with the strong red wine of his joy. For fifteen billion years God prepared a place where human consciousness and love might exist and be turned toward the divine Creator. Would it not be quite possible that three spiritually perceptive, seeking human beings might see some new light in the sky and hear a message about the Creator's entrance into creation? (See note 2 in chapter 1 concerning John Barrows and Frank Tipler, *The Anthropic Cosmological Principle* [Oxford: Oxford University Press, 1989].)

2. T. S. Eliot, "Journey of the Magi," *The Collected Poems, 1909–1962* (New York: Harcourt, Brace & World, 1963), 98.

3. Henry Van Dyke, *The Story of the Other Wise Man* (New York: Harper & Brothers, 1923). John Shea speaks of the significance of the Magi in a telling way in *Starlight: Beholding the Christmas Miracle All Year Long* (New York: Crossroads Publishing Company, 1992).

4. Author's translation of Johann Wolfgang von Goethe, *Faust*, 2.5.11835, altered to avoid sexist language.

5. Matthew 2:6. This prophecy is a combination of Micah 5:2 and 2 Samuel 5:2.

6. Eliot, "Journey of the Magi," 99.

Chapter 9: The Herod in Us All

1. W. H. Auden, *For the Time Being: A Christmas Oratorio* in *Religious Drama 1* (New York: Meridian Books, 1957), 61. Few passages express better the easy way with which we destroy the inner Christ child than these words of W. H. Auden.

2. Matthew 2:18; quoting Jeremiah 31:15.

3. Pinchas Lapide, *The Resurrection of Jesus: A Jewish Perspective* (Minneapolis: Augsburg Publishing House, 1983), 148.

4. Albert Einstein and Sigmund Freud, *Why War?* (Paris: International Institute of Intellectual Cooperation, 1933), quoted by Karl Menninger, *Man Against Himself* (New York: Harcourt, Brace, 1938), 411.

5. Alison Curry, "Tolerance," *Democracy in Action: Journal of the Institute for a Democratic Alternative for South Africa* (South Africa), 7, no. 1:7.

6. Personal conversation with Cardinal Suenens.

7. For further information about The Church of the Saviour, see Elizabeth O'Connor, *Servant Leaders, Servant Structures*, The Servant Leadership School, 1640 Columbia Road, N.W., Washington, D.C. 20009, 1991.

8. I have discussed the reality and mystery of evil in depth in *Discernment: A Study in Ecstasy and Evil* (New York: Paulist Press, 1978).

Chapter 10: Cosmic Tentacles of Brilliance

1. See my *God, Dreams, and Revelation: A Christian Interpretation of Dreams* (Minneapolis: Augsburg, 1991), 31–56, for an in-depth discussion of the Hebrew belief in the religious value of the dream-vision. See 81–98 for an analysis of the Greek belief in the Divine-human encounter.

2. Luke 2:14, altered to avoid sexist language.

3. The hymns are quoted from *The Hymnal of the Protestant Episcopal Church in the United States of America* (New York: Church Pension Fund, 1943). The number of the hymn cited and the number of the verse of the hymn are given in parentheses. Hymns nos. 21, 19, and 13 are altered to avoid sexist language.

4. Victor White, *God and the Unconscious* (Cleveland: The World Book Publishing Company, 1961), 203. I have added "[and angels]" since White writes elsewhere of angels.

5. See my *Resurrection: Release from Repression* (Mahwah, N.J.: Paulist Press, 1985).

6. In *God, Dreams, and Revelation* (Minneapolis: Augsburg Fortress, 1991), I have presented in great detail evidence that the most significant leaders of the early church believed that the Holy One of Israel continued to guide the church through dreams, visions, and revelations during its period of persecution. The same conviction was held by nearly all the leaders of the church as Christianity became the established religion of the empire.

7. A Methodist chaplain who attended this conference and a seminary student who heard it from Niemoller when he was a visiting professor told me of this account.

8. Nouwen's experience was first printed as an article titled "A Glimpse behind the Mirror: Reflections on Death and Life" in *Weavings, a Journal of Christian Spiritual Life* 4, no. 6 (November/December 1989): 13–23, and was later published in an expanded form in *Beyond the Mirror* (New York: Crossroad, 1990).

9. This account is included in my book *Afterlife* (New York: Crossroad, 1986), 100–101. If we are not open to such experiences, people will not tell them to us.

Chapter 11: Augustus Caesar and Jesus Crucified

1. Paraphrase of Luke 1:51–52 to make it more relevant to the contents of this chapter.
2. Luke 2:1–2.
3. In *Mystical Christianity: A Psychological Commentary on the Gospel of John* (New York: Crossroad, 1993), John Sanford makes an excellent case that some of Jesus' followers were well-educated and religiously sophisticated.
4. Matthew 8:20.
5. Bishop Lance Webb has written two fascinating and accurate novels of early Christian life, *Onesimus* and *Onesimus: Rebel and Saint*, bound together (New York: Nelson, 1991).
6. *The Book of Common Prayer* (New York: Oxford University Press, 1952).

Chapter 12: The Grand Finale

1. 1 Corinthians 15:19.
2. Henri Nouwen, *Beyond the Mirror* (New York: Crossroad, 1990), 52.
3. Mark 15:39; Matthew 27:54.
4. The references for these and the following words of Jesus from the cross are, respectively, Luke 23:34, 43; Matthew 27:46 and Mark 15:34; John 19:26–27, 28, 30; Luke 23:46. I have reflected on these words in depth in *Through Defeat to Victory: Stories and Meditations of Spiritual Rebirth* (Rockport, Mass.: Element, Inc., 1992) and in *The Cross: Meditations on the Seven Last Words of Christ* (New York: Paulist Press, 1980).
5. Mark 16:6–7. See *Resurrection: Release from Oppression* (Mahweh, N.J.: Paulist Press, 1985) for my reasons for the sequence in which I now tell the story of the resurrection of Jesus. I was moved to write this book after reading *The Man Born to Be King* (San Francisco: Ignatius Press, 1990) by Dorothy Sayers. Here this profound Christian and superb detective-story writer shows how the different accounts of the resurrection can be harmonized into a consecutive narrative.
6. John 20:17. According to many Greek scholars this is a more accurate translation of the Greek than that given in the NRSV. The preceding biblical references are based on John 20:13, 15, and 16, 17.
7. See Luke 24:13–49.
8. Taken from John 20:25–29.
9. John 21:15–17.
10. *The Hymnal of the Protestant Episcopal Church in the United States of America* (New York: Church Pension Fund, 1943), no. 354.
11. Acts 1:6–11.
12. In *Tongue Speaking: The History and Meaning of Charismatic Experiences* (New York: Crossroad, 1981), I have in detail described this experience and its continuing history throughout the ages of the church.
13. John Sanford, *Mystical Christianity* (New York: Crossroad, 1993, 329). In John's Gospel, Jesus speaks of the Paraclete or advocate that cannot come

until he leaves, another reference to some kind of separation (ascension) that took place between the disciples and the risen, yet earthly, Jesus.

14. John 1:1, 3–5, 14, 16. In *Mystical Christianity*, 1–27, John Sanford gives an exhaustive description of the meaning of the Greek word *logos*.

Chapter 13: Letting Christ into Our Lives

1. I have written in depth on each of these suggestions. On the subject of world view, I have written: *Reaching: The Journey to Fulfillment* (San Francisco: HarperCollins, 1990) and *Encounter with God* (Mahwah, N.J.: Paulist Press, 1987); on prayer and meditation, *The Other Side of Silence* (Mahwah, N.J.: Paulist Press, 1977); and on Christian journal-keeping, *Adventure Inward* (Minneapolis: Augsburg Fortress, 1980). I presented the story of the resurrection in *Resurrection: Release from Oppression* (Mahwah, N.J.: Paulist Press, 1985). On the subject of our need for psychological wisdom, I wrote *Christianity As Psychology* (Minneapolis: Augsburg Fortress, 1986). On the necessity and practice of love and caring, I present my views—and my own experience—in *Caring: How Can We Love One Another* (Mahwah, N.J.: Paulist Press, 1982). On the subjects of healing and religious experience in the Bible and Christian tradition, I have written *Psychology, Medicine and Christian Healing* (San Francisco: Harper Collins, 1986) and *God, Dreams and Revelation* (Minneapolis: Augsburg Fortress, 1991).

2. Fyodor Dostoyevski, *The Brothers Karamazov*, trans. Andrew R. MacAndrew (New York: Bantam Books, 1970), 2:66–67.